Front endsheet: Washington welcomed by the ladies of Trenton, New Jersey, in 1789; Library of Congress. Back endsheet: Signing of the Declaration of Independence; L. L. Bean Collection. Front cover: George Washington, Museum of Fine Arts, Boston; Martha Washington, National Gallery of Art, Mellon Collection; Washington crossing the Delaware, Mr. and Mrs. Bertram K. Little Collection; Benjamin Franklin, Historical Society of Pennsylvania. Back cover: Mount Vernon, National Gallery of Art, Gift of Edgar William and Bernice Chrysler Garbisch; John Adams jug, J. Doyle DeWitt Collection; Alexander Hamilton, The White House Collection; John Paul Jones, Independence Hall; Washington's telescope, Mount Vernon; Boston Tea Party, Colonial Williamsburg.

VOLUME

1

THE AMERICAN HERITAGE BOOK OF THE PRESIDENTS AND FAMOUS AMERICANS

★ ★ ★ ★ ★

GEORGE WASHINGTON
JOHN ADAMS

CREATED AND DESIGNED BY THE EDITORS OF
AMERICAN HERITAGE
The Magazine of History

12-VOLUME EDITION PUBLISHED BY
DELL PUBLISHING CO., INC., NEW YORK, N.Y.

THE AMERICAN HERITAGE
BOOK OF THE
PRESIDENTS AND FAMOUS AMERICANS

CREATED AND DESIGNED BY THE EDITORS OF
AMERICAN HERITAGE
The Magazine of History

PRESIDENT	James Parton
EDITORIAL COMMITTEE	Joseph J. Thorndike, *Chairman*
	Oliver Jensen
	Richard M. Ketchum
SENIOR EDITOR	Bruce Catton
SENIOR ART DIRECTOR	Irwin Glusker
EDITOR, GENERAL BOOKS	Alvin M. Josephy, Jr.
PUBLISHER	Darby Perry

Staff for this project

EDITOR	Kenneth W. Leish
ASSOCIATE EDITORS	David Jacobs
	Michael Harwood
PICTURE EDITOR	Wesley Day
ASSISTANT EDITORS	Nancy Kelly
	John Phillips
COPY EDITORS	Joan Wilkinson
	Brenda Bennerup
	Ellen C. Ehrlich
TEXT RESEARCHER	Susan D. Eikov
PICTURE RESEARCHER	Carla Davidson
ART DIRECTOR	Chester Prosinski

12-VOLUME EDITION PUBLISHED BY DELL PUBLISHING CO., INC.

PUBLISHER	George T. Delacorte
PRESIDENT	Mrs. Helen Meyer
EXECUTIVE VICE PRESIDENT	William F. Callahan, Jr.
VICE PRESIDENT	Carl W. Tobey
VICE PRESIDENT AND PROJECT DIRECTOR	Walter B. J. Mitchell, Jr.
PRODUCTION DIRECTOR	Rosalie Barrow
PROMOTION DIRECTOR	M. J. Jossel
SALES DIRECTOR	Joseph C. Penell

Copyright © 1967 by American Heritage Publishing Co., Inc., 551 Fifth Avenue, New York, New York 10017. All rights reserved under Berne and Pan-American Copyright Conventions. Library of Congress Catalogue Card Number: 67-12999.

COMPLETE CONTENTS OF TWELVE VOLUMES

VOLUME 1
George Washington
John Adams
15 Famous Americans

VOLUME 2
Thomas Jefferson
James Madison
James Monroe
22 Famous Americans

VOLUME 3
John Quincy Adams
Andrew Jackson
Martin Van Buren
13 Famous Americans

VOLUME 4
William H. Harrison
John Tyler
James K. Polk
Zachary Taylor
Millard Fillmore
7 Famous Americans

VOLUME 5
Franklin Pierce
James Buchanan
Abraham Lincoln
20 Famous Americans

VOLUME 6
Andrew Johnson
Ulysses S. Grant
Rutherford B. Hayes
21 Famous Americans

VOLUME 7
James A. Garfield
Chester A. Arthur
Grover Cleveland
Benjamin Harrison
25 Famous Americans

VOLUME 8
William McKinley
Theodore Roosevelt
William H. Taft
21 Famous Americans

VOLUME 9
Woodrow Wilson
Warren G. Harding
Calvin Coolidge
23 Famous Americans

VOLUME 10
Herbert C. Hoover
Franklin D. Roosevelt
24 Famous Americans

VOLUME 11
Harry S. Truman
Dwight D. Eisenhower
24 Famous Americans

VOLUME 12
John F. Kennedy
Lyndon B. Johnson
16 Famous Americans
Index

See Tables of Contents in each volume for listings of Famous Americans.

George Washington

John Adams

CONTENTS OF VOLUME ONE

FOREWORD BY BRUCE CATTON 6

GEORGE WASHINGTON 9
A PICTURE PORTFOLIO 27
FACTS IN SUMMARY 58

JOHN ADAMS 61
A PICTURE PORTFOLIO 71
FACTS IN SUMMARY 88

FAMOUS AMERICANS

Samuel Adams	74	John Paul Jones	38
George Rogers Clark	39	Henry Knox	49
Benjamin Franklin	77	Daniel Morgan	38
Nathanael Greene	39	James Otis	75
Alexander Hamilton	46	Thomas Pinckney	81
John Hancock	74	Edmund Randolph	49
John Jay	48	Paul Revere	75

James Wilson 48

FOREWORD
BY BRUCE CATTON

The highest and most significant office in the United States is of course the Presidency. It was created by the Founding Fathers, and since their day it has been developed, strengthened, and marvelously expanded until it is much greater than it was originally designed to be. It is the principal instrument through which the people of the United States try to control their destiny in a complicated and uncertain world. Perhaps the best way to examine the office is to examine the lives and personalities of the men who have held it, because the Presidency today is in many ways the sum of large and small contributions made by the different Presidents.

At this writing there have been thirty-five of these men, and they make a mixed grill. Sometimes it seems that they have nothing much in common except the fact that for one reason or another the voters elevated them to high office. Some of them were surpassingly strong men and some of them were woefully weak; some of them ideally fitted the times they served, a few were obviously miscast, and still others were simply average men doing the best they could in a most demanding job. Each man was in his own day the man to whom the country looked for leadership, and by and large the leadership has usually been forthcoming. If the story of the Presidents proves nothing else, it testifies to the enormous stability of the office itself and of the nation that devised it.

The country does not always elect its most famous and talented men to the Presidency. The list of prominent Americans who were highly qualified for the job but never got it is long. It can be balanced by a list of Presidents who would hardly be remembered today, except by the historians of political life, if they had not entered the White House. (Who would recall Millard Fillmore, John Tyler, Franklin Pierce, Chester Alan Arthur, or Benjamin Harrison?) There are, on the list, some very good men who were overwhelmed by the immense problems that the Presidency brought them: James Buchanan, Andrew Johnson, and Ulysses S. Grant, for instance, were dedicated men who simply

faced more than they knew how to handle. Often enough, a man who seems poorly qualified for the office grows mightily once he gets in it—Andrew Jackson, for example, and Abraham Lincoln, to name only two. A time of crisis does not always bring forth a President who can cope with crisis—a strong President or two in the decade just before the Civil War might have saved the country an infinity of suffering, and the same is true of the early 1920's—but surprisingly often we get a big man just when we need one.

Indeed, the most interesting thing about the long roll call of men who have lived in the White House is that the average is so surprisingly high. One of our favorite jokes has to do with the offhand way in which we choose our Vice Presidents. Logically, these men ought to be dismal failures when tragedy puts them into the top job. Actually, they are not. Some were ineffective Presidents to be sure, but some were genuinely first-rate.

One thing that stands out is that the office of the Presidency has always been growing—partly because the times themselves have demanded it, but also because certain exceptional men have stretched the powers of the office in order to do things that needed to be done for the nation. Jefferson, Jackson, Lincoln, the two Roosevelts, Truman: each of them made the office bigger by boldly exerting its implied but unstated powers. Bear in mind, too, that none of the men who seized and exercised the undefined authority that becomes visible to the man in the White House was guilty of anything like Caesarism. Every man who ever lived in the White House understood that he was acting for something much bigger than himself. When he reached out for additional authority, he was getting it for the Presidency and not for himself.

Here they are, then—the men who have been Presidents of the United States. They make a pretty good group, all in all, and they have not failed us. Only a nation with sound instincts for the survival of freedom, democracy, and the national well-being could have chosen a group that stands the backward glance as well as this one does.

THE FIRST PRESIDENT (1789–1797)

GEORGE WASHINGTON

George Washington, said an Antifederalist newspaper, has "the ostentation of an eastern bashaw." The first President, a contemporary senator insisted, "has become in the hands of Hamilton, the dishclout of every dirty speculation, as his name goes to wipe away blame and silence all murmuring." On the eve of Washington's retirement, Benjamin Franklin's grandson, Benjamin Bache, crowed: "Every heart . . . ought to beat high in exultation, that the name of Washington ceases from this day to give a currency to political iniquity and to legalize corruption."

Other opponents accused him of stealing from the Treasury, of toadying to the British, of being inept as a general. An embittered Tom Paine, imprisoned by the French for revolutionary agitation, condemned Washington's neutrality in his case: "As to you, sir, treacherous in private friendship . . . and a hypocrite in public life, the world will be puzzled to decide . . . whether you have abandoned good principles, or whether you ever had any."

To most of his contemporaries, however, George Washington—commander of the tattered colonial army, chairman of the Constitutional Convention, first President of the United States—was indisputably first in war, first in peace, and first in the hearts of his countrymen. Despite their political differences, Thomas Jefferson spoke for the nation in urging Washington to seek a second term: "The confidence of the whole Union is centered in you . . ." he told his chief. "North and South will hang together if they have you to hang on." After Washington's death, Jefferson wrote: "Never did nature and fortune combine more perfectly to make a man great, and to place him in . . . an everlasting remembrance."

But America would not be satisfied with the realities—glorious though they were—of Washington's life. It wanted a flawless hero. Washington "was des-

Washington at sixty-three, by Gilbert Stuart

tined to a stature in death," writes historian Daniel Boorstin, "which he had never attained in life.... A deification which in European history might have required centuries was accomplished here in decades."

Thus, despite the political slander and bile that marred Washington's two administrations, the first President soon came to be regarded as a demigod. Mason Locke Weems, an Episcopal clergyman and itinerant bookseller, reaped enormous profits from his largely apocryphal biography of Washington, first published in 1800. Weems attributed all virtues to the first President, from extraordinary honesty, bravery, and wisdom to exceptional physical dexterity; in the fifth edition of the biography, printed in 1806, the legend of Washington and the cherry tree first appeared in type. Despite Weems's crass assurance to his publisher that the latter had "a great deal of money lying in the bones of old George," the myths he spawned engaged and still engage Americans.

Because of this literature of hero worship, because of Washington's own reticence, and because of his family's penchant for burning, editing, or giving away his private papers and letters, the personality of George Washington has remained obscure, distant, never quite credible. Perhaps historian W. E. Woodward was partially correct when he wrote that people think they do not understand Washington because they can find in him nothing that is not within themselves. "It was just in that quality that his greatness lay. He was the American common denominator, the average man deified and raised to the nth power."

In any case, American history has made the arduous passage from Washington mythology to balanced fact. We no longer imagine, with a facetious Nathaniel Hawthorne, that Washington "was born with his clothes on, and his hair powdered, and made a stately bow on his first appearance in the world." Nor given contemporary scholarship can we fully agree that he remains, any longer, "the man almost nobody knows."

The first President of the United States was born in royal Virginia's Westmoreland

This mug, probably made in Germany in 1776, is believed by some scholars to present the earliest depiction of Washington cutting down the cherry tree.

County, in a brick farmhouse, at 10 A.M. on February 11, 1732 (or February 22, according to the modern calendar adopted in 1752). His father was Augustine Washington, "a blond giant," according to biographer James T. Flexner, "fabulously strong but miraculously gentle . . . a nervous businessman." Augustine's second wife, Mary Ball Washington, was the mother of George and his three brothers—Samuel, John Augustine, and Charles—and two sisters. George also had two half brothers, Lawrence and Augustine, Jr., and a half sister, Jane.

The Washington mythology—nurtured by Weems and others—idealized Mary Washington as the perfect American mother. In reality, however, she was querulous and illiterate, and resented George's success because she felt that he neglected her. She refused to participate in any ceremony honoring him, deprecated his achievements, and despite the commander in chief's ample provisions for her financial needs, actually asked the Virginia legislature, at the height of the Revolutionary War, to come to her aid—to Washington's anger and embarrassment.

Attended from birth by slaves, George first moved with his parents some forty miles up the Potomac to a 2,500-acre tract named Epsewasson (later Mount Vernon) and in 1738 to a smaller plot, Ferry Farm, on the Rappahannock. When George was eleven, his father died, and thereafter Mary Washington's eldest child escaped her watchful eye whenever he could, fleeing to visit relatives and friends.

"Some men," Washington observed, "will gain as much experience in the course of three or four years as some will in ten or a dozen." And if experience is the best teacher, President Washington was well taught indeed. His education—acquired from members of his family, and perhaps also from a private tutor and from schoolteachers in Fredericksburg and Westmoreland County —was rudimentary, limited to accounting, utilitarian arithmetic, geometry, geography as a basis of surveying, and practical studies of the calendar and the zodiac. He was thoroughly practical—"a man of hands," wrote Woodward, "not without brains, but with hand and brain moving together. . . . He used thought only as a mode of action."

Nevertheless, the young Washington did occasionally find time for Alexander Pope, the Bible, *Tom Jones*, and *The Spectator*. And a list of maxims for correct social behavior caught his copybook fancy: the *Rules of Civility*, probably prepared by sixteenth-century Jesuits for the cultivation of French aristocrats. The maxims suggested that acceptable social conduct does not include cleaning one's teeth with the tablecloth, that "every action done in company ought to be with some sign of respect to those that are present," and that the correct man will remember to "bedew no man's face with Spittle, by approaching too near."

It was this copybook ethic that Washington carried with him in his careful ascent in Virginia society. His patron and tutor in this rise was his half brother Lawrence. It was Lawrence's marriage to Anne Fairfax, of the wealthy Virginia Fairfaxes, and the couple's frequent sojourns at Belvoir, the huge estate of Anne's father, that opened the gates of wealth and status to young George. As Lawrence's protégé, he often visited Belvoir, where George Fairfax (Anne's brother) and his wife, Sally, had taken up residence.

At sixteen, Washington accompanied George Fairfax on a month-long surveying tour of Lord Thomas Fairfax's vast lands beyond the Blue Ridge in the Shenandoah Valley. For his efforts Washington was paid $7.20 per day, a tidy fee for the time. The lodgings made available to them on this trip were not all that Washington could have wished. Of one place, he noted: "I . . . strip[p]ed myself very orderly and went in to ye Bed as they called it when to my Surprize I found it to be nothing but a Little Straw— Matted together without Sheets or anything else but only one thread Bear blanket with double its Weight of Vermin, such as Lice Fleas & c . . . I put on my Cloth[e]s and Lay as my Companions."

Wherever he went, Washington already commanded attention by his mere physical presence. Six-foot-two, lanky, and large-

Lawrence Washington became mentor to his favorite half brother, George, when their father died.

MOUNT VERNON LADIES' ASSOCIATION

boned (he wore a size 13 shoe), he had gray-blue eyes and brown hair. "In conversation he looks you full in the face," Captain George Mercer observed in 1760, "is deliberate, deferential, and engaging. . . . His movements and gestures are graceful, his walk majestic, and he is a splendid horseman." Meticulous in counting his possessions, he once actually calculated the number of seeds in a pound (troy weight) of red clover: 71,000. And he knew every foot of land he owned (1,459 acres purchased with surveying wages before he was nineteen). A few years later, during the French and Indian War, he would say of himself: "I have a constitution hardy enough to encounter and undergo the most severe trials, and, I flatter myself the resolution to face what any man durst."

In 1751 George accompanied Lawrence Washington to Barbados, where his half brother, ill with tuberculosis, hoped to regain his health. There, George contracted the smallpox that pock-marked his face permanently, but fortunately left him immune to the disease that later ravaged his Continental Army. In the following year, Lawrence Washington died, and George began his military career.

Commissioned a major in the militia, Washington was appointed adjutant of the southern district of Virginia. In the fall of 1753 he was given a historic assignment by Governor Robert Dinwiddie: to carry to the French at Fort Le Boeuf, three hundred miles away in the Ohio Valley, a royal ultimatum to cease fortifications and settlements there "within His Majesty's Dominions." Washington left on his mission on November 15. He stopped on the way to survey the site of a projected fort and, at Logstown on the north bank of the Ohio, urged the Indians, unsuccessfully, to accept the British as benign big brothers. Proceeding to Le Boeuf, he found the French adamant and cocky in their rejection of Britain's claims.

Having recorded a careful description of the fort in his notebook, Washington headed for home, on a trek through the frozen wilderness that can only be called heroic. The horses, hampered by deep snow, were unable to proceed, and Washington and his guide, Christopher Gist, had to continue on foot, through Indian-infested forests, to Williamsburg, more than five hundred miles away. Near Murthering Town, close to the Forks of the Ohio, an Indian, perhaps a French hireling, fired point-blank at Washington at fifteen paces but missed.

Washington had hoped that the Allegheny River would be frozen solid when he and Gist reached it, but it was not; masses of ice were crashing down the river. With one hatchet between them, the two men built a raft at a spot now within Pittsburgh's city limits, and then launched it into the icy cascade. "Before we were halfway over," Washington wrote later, "we were jammed in the ice, in such a manner that we expected every

After his trek back to Virginia from Fort Le Boeuf in the winter of 1753–54, Washington wrote a chronicle of his mission that brought him some renown.

Washington's brass telescope, still at Mount Vernon

moment our raft to sink and ourselves to perish. I put out my setting pole to try to stop the raft that the ice might pass by, when the rapidity of the stream threw it [the raft] with such violence against the pole that it jerked me out into ten feet of water but I fortunately saved myself by catching hold of one of the raft logs." Drenched and shivering, the men continued their march, reaching Will's Creek, some fifty miles from Winchester, on January 7, 1754.

The defiant reply of the French confirmed Governor Dinwiddie's conviction that British holdings in the Ohio Valley must be defended. For Washington there was the pleasure of seeing his report officially printed, plus £50 voted him by a grateful Virginia assembly. He said of the money: "I was employed to go on a journey in the winter (when I believe few or none would have undertaken it), and what did I get by it? My expenses borne."

Commissioned a lieutenant colonel by Dinwiddie in 1754, Washington was ordered back to the Ohio Valley to secure the site of the Ohio Company's fort, which was being built at the junction of the Allegheny and Monongahela rivers. En route he learned that the site had fallen to the French (they named it Fort Duquesne), and that enemy troops were advancing toward him in strength. At Great Meadows, Pennsylvania, Washington's men surrounded and attacked a party of French soldiers without warning. Ten Frenchmen, including their chief officer, Joseph Coulon, the Sieur de Jumonville, were killed and twenty-one were captured.

Washington then entrenched at an abandoned fort he named "Necessity." It was "badly sited," notes historian Esmond Wright, "in an open, swampy hollow over which a nearby hill gave a commanding view." This was the first of several less-than-brilliant maneuvers that would earn for Washington the criticism of some military strategists. On July 3, a superior force, led by Jumonville's brother, compelled Washington to surrender and, taking advantage of the Virginian's ignorance of French, obtained his signature on a written admission that he had "assassinated" Jumonville.

Washington's hasty action in attacking the French party is sometimes credited with precipitating the Seven Years' War. But for Washington it would be indispensable experience in frontier military tactics, and a source of notoriety in the chancelleries of Europe. Disillusioned with what he considered Dinwiddie's mismanagement of Virginia's military establishment, and bitter because of a ruling that colonials could not rise above the rank of captain in the British army, Washington resigned his commission at the end of 1754.

After the Fort Necessity fiasco, Washington wrote: "I have heard the bullets whistle; and, believe me, there is something charming in the sound." But the bullets lost their charm in 1755. In May, Washington was appointed aide-de-camp to General Edward Braddock in a 1,300-man expedition against Fort Duquesne. At the Monongahela they met a French and Indian force. Braddock's men, trained in traditional European methods of battle, were surrounded and decimated by enemies adept at frontier warfare. Braddock himself was slain, and sixty-three of his eighty-six officers were killed or wounded. The regulars panicked and fled; according to Washington, the Virginia colonials alone "behaved like men and died like soldiers." Washington himself had two horses killed under him, and four bullets pierced his coat before he organized a retreat.

Returning to Virginia, Washington was named a colonel and commander in chief of the militia. He was thus called upon, at twenty-three, to defend the colony's 300-mile frontier from what was considered an imminent French and Indian attack. But inadequate troops and provisions, limited authority, and a royal governor who would not give him permission to seize Fort Duquesne, the key position in the West, made his task impossible. When even his right to command was challenged by an officer of the Maryland militia who held a royal commission, Washington rode all the way from Williamsburg to Boston to ask Governor William Shirley, the acting commander in chief of British forces in North America, to confirm his rank. In Boston, the proud young colonel was told to his great satisfaction that his rank was valid, though only when no British regulars were present.

For more than two years, Washington doggedly defended Virginia's long frontier with ill-equipped, unpaid militiamen. Then, in 1758, a British force under General John Forbes was assigned to march on Fort Duquesne. Washington was selected to serve as Forbes's acting brigadier, and when the French abandoned and burned the fort, the main objective of his strategy for Virginia's defense was achieved. He resigned his commission and retired to sixteen years of publicly uneventful but privately joyous life.

Washington's marriage to the widow Martha Dandridge Custis on January 6, 1759, vastly increased his fortune. Plump and appealing, and reputedly the richest widow in the colony, Martha Washington added 17,000 acres to George's 5,000, and 300 slaves to his 49. She also provided him with a town house in the capital at Williamsburg and with Daniel Custis' two children, the overindulged and indolent John Parke Custis and the epileptic Martha Parke Custis, who died at seventeen.

Martha Washington was good-natured, healthy, and prosaic. With the assistance of thirteen servants and seven workmen, she kept a fine household at Mount Vernon, which Washington leased from Lawrence's heirs until he inherited it in 1761. George called Martha "Patsy," and Martha, twenty-seven at the time of the marriage, called George, twenty-six, "Old Man." That their marriage was based primarily on love is unlikely. Indisputably, Washington had earlier fallen in love with George Fairfax's wife, Sally, the coquettish belle of the Williamsburg cotillions. On July 20, 1758, he had assured Martha, as a "faithful and affectionate friend," that her life was "now inseparable from [his]," recalling "that happy hour when we made our pledges to each other." Less than two months later, he directly avowed by letter his love for Mrs. Fairfax. "The world has no business to know the object of my love, declared in this manner to you," wrote the affianced soldier, "when I want to conceal it." There is no evidence that the love was consummated or that Martha knew of it. But his letters to Sally remain. Not all the glories of the Revolutionary command, nor even the splendors of the Presidency, Washington assured Sally near the end of his life, had "been able to eradicate from my mind those happy moments, the happiest of my life, which I have enjoyed in your company."

Nevertheless, he settled down with Martha at Mount Vernon and became a dutiful vestryman and church warden, punctual tobacco planter, land broker, speculator, and surveyor. Now one of the richest men in Virginia, Washington—in historian Shelby Little's words—"took up his duties as a Burgess, was publicly thanked for his great services to his country, and drafted a law to prevent hogs running at large in Winchester." From 1768 to 1774 he also served as a Fairfax County justice.

Everyone at Mount Vernon knew his place. "Mrs. Forbes," Washington said of his housekeeper, "will have a warm, decent and comfortable room to herself, to lodge in, and will eat of the Victuals of our Table, but not sit at it, at any time, *with us*, be her appearance what it may: for if this was *once admitted*, no line satisfactory to either party,

Mrs. Sally Fairfax, a Virginia neighbor, was the object of Washington's discreet but lifelong love.

perhaps, could be drawn thereafter." Welcome at the table or not, Mrs. Forbes had her hands full. Washington entertained lavishly in the tradition of the Virginia gentry, despite his complaint that his house was, at times, "a well resorted tavern."

He carefully supervised every detail of plantation production and management: accounts receivable and payable, mortgage payments due, the state of the crops and fertilizing experiments, the performance of brood mares. When he had time, he read books such as *A New System of Agriculture or a Speedy Way to Grow Rich*.

Washington's attitude toward his Negro slaves at first reflected that of the reigning plantation owners of his time. Slaves were property, efficient or not. His viewpoint changed, however. In the early 1770's he committed himself to the gradual abolition of the slave trade through legislation. Although he owned more slaves than he needed, he refused to sell them without their permission. Drawing a parallel between the tyranny of slavery and the tyranny of Britain toward the colonies, he nevertheless opposed freeing slaves who were content with their masters. Such action, he argued, would lead to "discontent on one side and resentment on the other."

Though an Anglican vestryman, Washington was not religious in a formal sense. On one occasion, however, he assured Sally Fairfax that "there is a Destiny which has the control of our actions not to be resisted by the strongest efforts of Human Nature." He willingly granted to all the right to travel "that road to heaven which to them shall seem the most direct, plainest, easiest, and least liable to exceptions."

By 1774, Washington had begun to participate actively in America's burgeoning economic and political revolution. He had opposed the Stamp Act and thoroughly approved Massachusetts' refusal to submit to British commercial restrictions. Angered by Britain's retaliatory closing of the port of Boston, he was present with Jefferson at the Raleigh Tavern in Williamsburg on May 27, 1774, after the Crown had dissolved the rebellious House of Burgesses. At this meeting, the Virginia legislators issued a vote of sympathy with their New England brothers, appointed delegates to a Virginia convention that would select representatives to a continental congress, and passed a resolution stating that an attack on one of the colonies would be considered an attack on all of them. Later that year, Washington was chosen to attend the First Continental Congress in Philadelphia, at which he sat silently but impressively, his sword at his side.

After being elected to command five Virginia militia companies, Washington was appointed a delegate to the Second Continental Congress of May, 1775; there he served on a committee charged with drafting regulations for a colonial army and a strategy for the defense of New York City. In that Second Congress, John Adams of Massachusetts nominated George Washington as commander in chief of a proposed Continental Army. He was elected unanimously. In assuming the post, Washington was humbly

Washington, painted in 1776 by C. W. Peale

magnanimous: "Though I am truly sensible of the high honor done me in this appointment, yet I feel great distress from a consciousness that my abilities and military experience may not be equal to the extensive and important trust." But he would accede to Congress' will, do his plain duty, and "exert every power I possess in the service for support of the glorious cause." Refusing a salary, he asked only that Congress bear his expenses.

In his General Orders, issued the next day, Washington appealed for a unified effort to end regionalism and colonial jealousies. Throughout the war, from the siege of Boston to Yorktown, he would be frustrated by the very sectionalism he abjured; by recalcitrant governors more concerned with their colonies' defenses than with those of the emerging nation; by chronic desertions, inadequate arms, desperately bad food and provisions, unreliable intelligence, and mercantile profiteering; and by limited terms of conscription that prolonged the war and increased the cost of training troops.

Washington took command of his troops in Cambridge, Massachusetts, on July 3, 1775. Lack of ammunition and cannon, however, delayed his first major move until March, 1776, when he fortified Dorchester Heights, placing Boston and the British fleet in the port under threat of bombardment. The British evacuated the city on March 17, and Washington, having received an honorary doctorate from Harvard, led his troops to New York City, where, he correctly believed, the enemy would strike next.

In New York, Washington had 20,000 ill-trained troops. With them, he was expected to beat back a combined British assault force—then gathering at Staten Island—of some 32,000 crack redcoats under General William Howe and more than 30 war vessels and 400 transports under Sir William's brother, Admiral Richard Howe.

On July 4, 1776, a jubilant Congress proclaimed in the Declaration of Independence that the colonies were free of the Crown under "the Laws of Nature and of Nature's God." But in August, the brothers Howe moved in to seize control of New York Harbor and both the East and Hudson rivers. Facing encirclement, Washington dispatched 5,000 men to Brooklyn Heights, maintaining the rest of his forces in Manhattan.

William Howe defeated the colonials in the Battle of Long Island, inflicting 1,500 casualties. The Howes failed, however, to follow through by sailing up the East River and cutting Washington's forces in two. On August 29, Washington withdrew the rest of his Long Island troops to Manhattan.

Plagued by desertions, Washington's forces dwindled, while British ranks swelled. In September, Howe struck again in a massive landing at Kip's Bay, and facing no opposition from the terrified and retreating colonials (who earned Washington's cane-swinging rage), forced Washington north to Harlem Heights. When Congress rejected his proposal to burn New York, Washington stationed 7,500 men to guard the Hudson at both Fort Washington on the New York shore and Fort Lee on the New Jersey side. He then eluded Howe's advance up the East River by retreating to White Plains in October. Attacked there, he retreated again.

In November, Washington proceeded to Fort Lee only to see it captured by General Charles Cornwallis' troops, who scaled the

Palisades. (The British had taken Fort Washington two days earlier.) With 5,000 men, Washington retreated through New Jersey and crossed the Delaware into Pennsylvania. The British, now in firm control of New York City and most of New Jersey, sent a portion of their force to pursue him, garrisoning finally at Trenton and Bordentown. "I am wearied almost to death," Washington said. "I think the game is pretty near up."

But now, as at so many times when conditions seemed hopeless, Washington moved with daring and grandeur. On Christmas night, 1776, he and his men rowed silently across the ice-laden Delaware River to attack the sleeping encampment of British mercenaries at Trenton. The attack, in which some nine hundred Hessians were taken prisoner, constituted a major turning point in the war, the first of Washington's justly celebrated surprise maneuvers.

After the British captured Fort Washington, New York, in 1776, they moved to take Fort Lee, on the New Jersey side of the Hudson. Some 4,000 soldiers (below) crossed the river, climbed the Palisades, and just missed trapping the garrison, which fled.

Undeterred, a confident Lord Cornwallis moved toward Washington's new headquarters at Trenton's Assunpink Creek. Again Washington played the fox, leaving his Trenton campfires burning throughout the night of January 2, 1777, and moving to Princeton, where he surprised and routed a British garrison, cutting Cornwallis' line of supply. As the British pulled back to New York, Washington set up winter quarters in Morristown. He could well be proud, for in two spectacular moves he had regained most of New Jersey against vastly superior odds.

For their part, the British now resolved on a major new strategy: a thrust from Lake Champlain in the north to secure New England and New York, and to keep Washington busy on two fronts. But at Saratoga, 6,000 British troops under General John Burgoyne were defeated by some 17,000 Continentals led by General Horatio Gates. It was another turning point in the war, one that would rank with Yorktown.

The troops under Washington, however, faced a new period of despair. Howe, instead of coming to the aid of Burgoyne on Gates's southern flank, had chosen to take Philadelphia. Washington, with 10,500 troops,

marched south to meet Howe's 15,000 redcoats at Brandywine Creek on September 11, 1777. The Americans suffered 1,000 casualties in a clear defeat, but made an orderly retreat across the Schuylkill River. Howe entered Philadelphia on September 26. On October 4, in a daring if unsuccessful assault, Washington attacked Howe's main encampment at Germantown, Pennsylvania, and after losing 1,000 more men, retired for the winter to Valley Forge, twenty miles outside Philadelphia.

It was a black season for General Washington. Valley Forge was, he said, "a dreary kind of place, and uncomfortably provided." It was a vast understatement. His men faced bitter cold and frost without shoes or blankets, were forced to drink soup "full of burnt leaves and dirt," and wore lice-ridden clothes, while the British fattened and wined on Pennsylvania Dutch largesse. Before the winter was over, 3,000 of Washington's 9,000 men had deserted. As if bitter hardship in the field was not a great enough burden, Washington was also attacked in Congress. Epitomizing the prevailing hypercritical mood was Jonathan Sargent's diatribe: "Thousands of Lives & Millions of property are yearly sacrificed to the Insufficiency of our Commander-in-Chief. . . ." But the British failure to attack Valley Forge allowed Washington's war-torn force to recover and to train.

In May, 1778, General Howe was replaced by Sir Henry Clinton, who left Philadelphia in June to march back through New Jersey to New York. Washington, in pursuit, met the British on June 28 at Monmouth, New Jersey, and held the field after angrily quashing a precipitate retreat of American forces under General Charles Lee. He then saw the British use one of his treasured tactics—withdrawal by night (to New York). Monmouth was the last major battle in the North. In February, 1778, the colonists received important news: France, impressed by the American victory at Saratoga, had entered the war in alliance with the colonies.

As Clinton initiated a series of hit-and-run raids in the North, the main British campaign under Cornwallis shifted to the South: Savannah was captured; an amphibious assault launched on Charleston took that city; and South Carolina was overrun as one of the worst American defeats took place at Camden on August 16, 1780. After a series of hard-fought battles in the South in the first half of 1781, Cornwallis marched to Virginia, where he brought his full force into Yorktown on August 1.

In the North, Washington's 9,000 Continentals were joined in 1781 by 7,800 French troops under the Comte de Rochambeau. A combined operation with the Comte de Grasse, the French naval commander in the West Indies, was planned for August. The objective: to trap Cornwallis by land and sea. Washington planned the march to Virginia skillfully, and when the French and American armies arrived there, Cornwallis found himself outnumbered two to one. French naval victories and the Franco-American siege convinced Cornwallis that his position was hopeless; he surrendered on October 17, 1781. It was the last major military engagement of the war.

What of Washington as military strategist and commander? It is clear that he made tactical blunders and that many of his contemporaries thought him too indecisive and too imperious for a republican commander. It is also true that he owed much to France, notably at Yorktown. But, the fact remains that Washington won the war.

Esmond Wright has written that "the explanation is not that Washington won [the war] but that Britain lost it, and to the terrain rather than to the enemy." But Washington won on many positive counts. He had unassailable and unflinching courage when it was needed most; the worst conditions brought out his best, in daring and in leadership. He believed in the "glorious cause" of America and, in the darkest moments, could envision its future greatness. And it is incontestable from contemporary descriptions that he possessed charisma, the magnetic aura of leadership that sways men.

On a purely military level he won because he knew his enemies and avoided meeting them on their terms. Faced with the disciplined ranks of Britain's troops, he concluded early: "We should on all occasions avoid a general action, nor put anything to the risk unless compelled by a necessity into which we ought never to be drawn." Accordingly, he became a master of tactical retreat, maneuver at night, and surprise attack.

Three extramilitary events reveal Washington's character and thinking during the Revolutionary period: the notorious Conway Cabal; Washington's firm rejection of a crown in an American monarchy; and his writing of the "Circular Letter to the Governors of All the States."

After his defeat of Burgoyne at Saratoga, General Gates enjoyed a seasonal glamour and applause. He became the focus of opposition to Washington's leadership. In 1777, the year of Gates's victory, Major General Thomas Conway, an Irish-born French officer serving with the colonial troops, wrote to Gates suggesting that the latter might well replace the "weak" Washington. The letter reached Washington, who simply informed Conway that he was aware of the latter's machinations. Further plotting prompted an avowal of congressional support for Washington, and Conway's schemes were aborted. Throughout the intrigue, Washington retained full self-control. Let generals who will, fight for status, he said. As for himself, he had only "one great end in view," the success of the Revolution.

After Yorktown, the unpaid Continental Army seethed over the public's ingratitude and neglect; civil affairs in 1782 bordered on anarchy. Washington was urged by a distinguished Philadelphia colonel, Lewis Nicola, to accept an American crown and thus mend the nation's sundered political fabric with a strong and popular monarchy. The General's reply to Nicola was prompt and vigorous: "Such ideas . . . I must view with abhorrence and reprehend with severity."

Washington's famed "Circular Letter to the Governors of All the States," written from Newburgh, New York, on June 8, 1783, is one of his very few formal statements of political philosophy. Noting the nation's great potential, Washington informed each of the states that if the nation's democratic experiment failed, only Americans could be blamed. "This is the time of their political probation," he wrote, ". . . this is the moment to establish or ruin their national Character for ever." He warned that a weak and eccentric union would enable European states to divide and conquer the country. To secure a more durable union, he advocated four "Pillars on which the glorious Fabrick of our Independency and National Character must be supported." These were "1st. An indissoluble Union of the States under an Federal Head. 2dly. A sacred regard to Public Justice. 3dly. The adoption of a proper Peace Establishment, and 4thly. The prevalence of that pacific and friendly Disposition, among the People of the United States, which will induce them to forget their local prejudices and policies, to make those mutual concessions which are requisite to the general prosperity, and in some instances, to sacrifice their individual advantages to the interest of the Community."

Washington himself set April 19, 1783, the anniversary of the Battle of Lexington, as the date of formal cessation of hostilities with England. He entered New York in triumph in November, welcomed by fireworks and waving flags. After toasting his retiring

Washington's mess chest, at right, was used by his orderlies to prepare his meals in the field.

officers' health at Fraunces' Tavern, he proceeded to Philadelphia, where he settled his expense account with Congress (declaring himself the loser) and resigned his commission at Annapolis in December.

Washington returned to Mount Vernon, his great mission accomplished. "At length," he said at fifty-one, "I am become a private citizen on the banks of the Potomac." He described himself as "a wearied traveller" who had "escaped the quicksands and mires which lay in his way." But he would know no retirement. The Articles of Confederation were proving wholly inadequate to the purposes of liberated colonies seeking union. Like other wealthy landowners and merchants, Washington was alarmed by a government unable to enforce its will, and shocked by such anarchic defiance of government as Shays' (anti-tax, anti-hard-money) Rebellion in Massachusetts. "Combustibles in every state," Washington said, needed only a spark to ignite the land.

In May, 1787, the Constitutional Convention met at Philadelphia. Among the delegates was George Washington of Virginia, who was welcomed to the city by enthusiastic crowds; on May 25 he was unanimously chosen president of the Convention.

If he had expressed hopes for a strong central government as a private citizen, in his new position Washington maintained an immaculate neutrality. Above fray and faction, he presided over the Convention with a grave and paternal silence, "a commanding witness to duty," as Clinton Rossiter has written, a hero "whose presence would raise hopes and quiet fears everywhere."

Washington's sole speech at the Convention urged the adoption of a ratio of 1 to 30,000, rather than 1 to 40,000, in House representation as more adequate "security for the rights and interests of the people." He also cast his vote for a strong Presidency.

Franklin said that often during the Constitutional Convention he had looked at the sun painted on Washington's chair (right) and had wondered if it implied dawn or dusk for the states. The signing of the Constitution convinced him it was a rising sun.

Then, having lent his enormous prestige to the new instrument of government, he returned to Mount Vernon to await the Constitution's ratification, believing it would "probably produce no small influence on the happiness of society through a long succession of ages to come."

With the Constitution ratified (New Hampshire's vote accomplished this on June 21, 1788), the United States had a strong federal government with authority to tax, to make its acts binding on the states, and to conduct foreign relations. Now once again the call went out to Mount Vernon. On February 4, 1789, the electoral college unanimously named George Washington the nation's first President. His Vice President was John Adams, the Northern half of the first balanced ticket. On April 16, Washington left his plantation for the nation's capital, then New York City. Despite his assurance that he had no "wish beyond that of living and dying an honest man on my own farm," he was now called, at the age of fifty-seven,

This medal commemorates an Indian treaty of 1792.

to lead a great experiment in democracy. He assumed the Presidency with no less foreboding than pride: "My movements to the chair of government," he said, "will be accompanied by feelings not unlike those of a culprit, who is going to the place of his execution." He had the comfort of knowing, however, that a hopeful, united nation stood by his side. Indeed, Pierce Butler, a Convention delegate, had written that the powers of the Presidency were "greater than I was disposed to make them. Nor . . . do I believe they would have been so great had not many of the members cast their eyes towards General Washington as President. . . ."

The President-elect was besieged by public applause, parades, and celebrations in a triumphal march from Mount Vernon to the capital. In New York, on April 30, 1789, Washington rode to Federal Hall, at the corner of Wall and Nassau streets, for the nation's first presidential inauguration. A jubilant, awed, and expectant crowd massed in the streets, looking up to the canopied portico, awaiting their champion and leader.

Then he appeared, majestic and tall, dressed in brown broadcloth and white silk stockings, his dress sword at his side. Robert Livingston, Chancellor of New York, lifted the Bible to administer the oath, which the Commander in Chief repeated, according to a newspaper account, with "devout fervency." Now President of the United States, Washington bowed to kiss the Bible. Then Chancellor Livingston said: "It is done," and shouted, "Long live George Washington, President of the United States!"

To both houses of Congress, assembled in the Senate chamber, Washington delivered the first Inaugural Address, his "aspect grave, almost to sadness," said one observer. Acceding once again to the nation's summons from the "asylum" of Mount Vernon, the President deprecated his "inferior endowments from nature." Invoking God's aid, declining a salary, and asking—again—only for his expenses, Washington expressed the hope that ". . . no local prejudices or attachments, no separate views nor party animosities, will misdirect the comprehensive and equal eye" that ought to govern the nation above sectional interests. Liberty and "the republican model of government," he said, are "*finally* staked on the experiment intrusted to the hands of the American people."

Washington wished to be a President above politics, above sectionalism, and, indeed, above all controversy. During his first administration he made nonpolitical tours of the thirteen states, North and South, in a symbolic gesture of American unity. He avoided all direct personal advocacy or involvement in congressional legislation and limited his messages to Congress to broad and optimistic homilies. But his hope of remaining completely above the fray was dashed by both Federalist and Republican opposition. Exasperated with Washington's sometimes glacial aloofness, John Adams called him "an old mutton head," and even Jefferson said on one occasion, "Curse on his virtues, they have undone his country."

But in the beginning there were only accolades, as George and Martha put in order the presidential office and household. Meanwhile, Congress debated what to call the new Chief Executive. The Senate, harried by its monarchist faction, debated the merits of "His Elective Majesty," "His Elective Highness," "His Highness, the President of the United States and Protector of the Rights of the Same," even "His Mighti-

President Washington had three executive mansions. In New York he lived first on Cherry Street (left), then on lower Broadway (center); in Philadelphia his home was on High Street (right). The White House, begun in 1792, was occupied in 1800.

ness." A more rational House of Representatives settled the matter. The Chief Executive would be styled, with elegant simplicity, "President of the United States."

Washington was acutely conscious of his immense power in setting precedents: "It is devoutly wished on my part," he said, "that these precedents may be fixed on true principles." If he made the wrong appointments as Chief Executive, he feared he "might perhaps raise a flame of opposition that could not easily, if ever, be extinguished. . . ." He believed that government officials should be appointed with rigorous care, on the basis of aptitude, residence, and "former merits and sufferings in the service." They should also be, he insisted, "just and candid men who are disposed to measure matters on a Continental Scale." In a bid for national unity, he appointed both Federalists and Antifederalists, with evident regard for geographic balance.

As his Secretary of State, Washington appointed Thomas Jefferson of Virginia, an ardent republican, Francophile, and democratic theorist. New York's Alexander Hamilton, Washington's Revolutionary aide-de-camp and confidant, and a major author of *The Federalist*, became Secretary of the Treasury. Henry Knox of Massachusetts, his artillerist in the Revolution, was named Secretary of War, and Edmund Randolph, another of Washington's aides-de-camp and a prime mover in Virginia's ratification of the Constitution, was appointed Attorney General.

Washington believed that "the Constitution of the United States, and the laws made under it, must mark the line of [his] official conduct. . . ." He would, he wrote, neither stretch presidential powers "nor relax from them in any instance whatever, unless imperious circumstances shd. render the measure indispensable." Nevertheless, Washington had no qualms about asserting firm presidential authority in areas where the Constitution was silent or gray. The Constitution said nothing about a Cabinet of appointed officers, but Washington named a Cabinet—and a strong one. Nor did the Constitution say anything about the President's right to proclaim neutrality (clearly a negative corollary to Congress' power to declare war), but Washington nonetheless did so during the Franco-British war. Personally, or through subordinates, he was a strong President, asserting executive priority as the occasion demanded and as the law, positively or tacitly, allowed.

Of Washington's methods as Chief Executive, Jefferson later said: "His mind . . . was slow in operation . . . but sure in conclu-

sion.... Hearing all suggestions, he selected whatever was best ... [but was] slow in readjustment." Neither hatred nor friendship, Jefferson added, could bias his decisions.

Deferential to Congress, Washington believed that a bill should be vetoed only if it were clearly unconstitutional. He had a rigid sense of the nation's tripartite system of checks and balances, but he had equal regard for his own presidential prerogatives. When an angry House of Representatives, controlled by Jefferson's Democratic-Republican party, demanded in 1796 that the President submit for its investigation all executive instructions and papers relating to Jay's controversial treaty with England, Washington reminded the House that its assent to this, or any treaty, was not legally required.

In a nation with no experience in strong elected executives, he worked slowly toward a presidential balance of dignity and candor. He believed that the President must in his "public character ... maintain the dignity of Office, without subjecting himself to the imputation of superciliousness."

When, on a visit to Massachusetts, Washington was invited to call on Governor John Hancock, he maintained his national priority with cool courtesy: "The President of the United States," he wrote to Hancock, "presents his best respects to the Governor, and has the honor to inform him that he shall be at home, 'till 2 o'clock." Washington's response to Hancock was supremely right. The President grasped—and grasped early—a central fact of American democracy: the President is not only elected by all the people, he embodies all the people. He is their ultimate representative.

This same conviction, reinforced by Washington's own patrician experience as a Virginia landowner, dictated a substantial degree of ritual pomp. Washington had no hesitation in forcing respect for the Presidency among European observers by moving through the capital in a yellow chariot adorned with gilded cupids and his coat of arms. The Executive Mansion, staffed by fourteen white servants and seven slaves, was managed with comparable splendor. Through doors opened by powdered and liveried lackeys, dignitaries and visitors moved twice weekly to the President's afternoon receptions and to "Lady" Washington's glacially formal levees.

Not all Americans were delighted by this display of executive elegance. The Antifederalists regarded the splendor as a harbinger of a new monarchy and aristocracy that had no place in buckskinned America. For their part, the Washingtons paid little heed to the clamor. They were learning that in assuming public stature they had relinquished all privacy. Besides, the new President had more on his mind than petty objections to his style of living. "There is a rank due to the United States among nations," he said, "which will be withheld, if not absolutely lost, by the reputation of weakness." It was on building the nation's strength that Washington concentrated. To sustain the new government, to secure the faith and allegiance of the nation's owning and controlling classes and of its farmers, laborers, and artisans, Washington knew he must first establish a strong financial system that would guarantee American money and credit and protect manufacture and trade.

The organization of America's basic financial structure was assigned to Alexander Hamilton, whose importance in the administration was second only to Washington's. Hamilton moved with swift efficiency to build his new system. In a deal with Jefferson and Madison, leaders of the Democratic-Republicans, he agreed to support the location of the new national capital on the Potomac, closer to the South, in exchange for the Virginians' approval of the federal government's assumption of state debts as a means of strengthening the central government. Hamilton also proposed that new bonds be issued, covering the federal debt at full value, and that a portion of the government's revenue be set aside regularly for payment of interest and principal.

In 1791, Hamilton suggested that the government form a corporation, the Bank of the United States, to issue bank notes backed by gold and silver as the official United States currency, and to serve as both the main depository of government funds and as the financial agent of the Treasury. It was to be a corporation supervised by the government but run by directors representing private stockholders. When agrarians and states' righters cried out against financial and political tyranny, and questioned Congress' constitutional right to charter a bank, Hamilton replied that this right was inherent in its power to tax, to regulate trade, and to defend the nation. In 1791, Washington signed the bill chartering the Bank. Also under Hamilton's aegis, a decimally based currency was adopted, an excise tax was imposed on whisky, and a protective tariff was adopted to favor domestic goods.

The Jeffersonians were incensed, Jefferson himself close to resignation over what he regarded as a flagrant collusion of financial and political oligarchies. Futilely Washington urged an end to both Hamilton's and Jefferson's "wounding suspicions and irritable charges," which had now reached a state of public vituperation. In 1792, however, both men agreed that only Washington's decision to accept a second term could even temporarily bridge the widening schism; Washington was unanimously re-elected.

The temper of the new federal government was tested by three events during Washington's second administration: the celebrated Whisky Rebellion; the machinations of the licentious Girondist French minister, Edmond Genêt; and the fierce public storm over John Jay's treaty with England.

In July, 1794, Washington was challenged by defiant whisky distillers in western Pennsylvania who abhorred the Federalist excise tax on their product. (It was difficult and expensive to transport corn to market, but when distilled into whisky, it became an easily movable cash crop—and their chief source of income.) They terrorized excise agents, forced troops guarding the chief excise inspector to surrender, and threatened to march on Pittsburgh. Alarmed that the revolt might spread, Washington called for some 15,000 state militiamen to check the insurgents and thus prove that the United States was "able [and] willing to support our government and laws." He and Hamilton both rode out to review the militia. There was little opposition to this demonstration of executive strength.

Throughout Washington's tenure as President, revolutionary France and its conflict with England remained as divisive an issue as Hamilton's fiscal programs. Washington's own policy was a formal and circumspect neutrality. But the tension was heightened in 1793 by the arrival in the United States of a new French minister, Citizen Edmond Genêt, who was messianically committed to recruiting American money and volunteers for France against Britain and gaining an advantageous commercial treaty for his

This Federalist cartoon has Washington and his troops marching out to meet an invasion by French republican "cannibals," while Jefferson, giving orders to his friends in a French accent, tries to impede the advance.

country. Playing on American antipathy toward Britain, the flamboyant Genêt harangued the populace and hired and armed United States privateers to prey on British ships and return them as prizes to American ports. "Ten thousand people in the streets of Philadelphia," said John Adams, "day after day threatened to drag Washington out of his house, and effect a revolution in the Government, or compel it to declare war in favor of the French revolution. . . ."

Washington and Hamilton, unmoved by the anti-British sentiment, were enraged by Genêt's activities. And when he threatened to appeal to the people for support (over Washington's head), even Jefferson, the Francophile, was upset. Washington demanded the minister's recall, but Genêt, fearful of returning to France (now under Jacobin control), appealed for and was granted asylum in the United States.

Despite Washington's firm declaration of neutrality, the British continued to impress American seamen and search United States ships on the pretext of hunting for deserters. They also continued to occupy military posts they had promised to abandon, and to incite the Indians to harass the Western frontier. The Maine-Canada boundary was also in dispute, as was the exclusion of American ships from West Indian trade.

To settle these issues, Washington sent Chief Justice John Jay to London in April, 1794. The contents of Jay's Treaty were not made public until March, 1795. Britain agreed to abandon the frontier military posts by 1796, to open her East and West Indian ports, to refer the Maine boundary dispute to a commission, and to negotiate ship-seizure claims, but she made no concession on trading rights, impressment, or the incitement of Indians. Moreover, the United States was denied the right to export many vital products to the West Indies.

The public and press exploded in wrath. Hamilton was stoned in the streets. The attacks on the treaty were aimed directly at Washington, phrased, said the President, in "such exaggerated and indecent terms as could scarcely be applied to a Nero, a notorious defaulter, or even to a common pickpocket." But Washington's prestige enabled him to withstand the assault. He signed the treaty in August, 1795. In another—more popular—treaty, with Spain, Washington secured the right of navigation on the Mississippi and the right to export from New Orleans duty-free for a period of three years.

In 1796, angered by Republican attacks and disillusioned by the calumny and abuses of the public, Washington reshuffled his Cabinet. After Jefferson and Hamilton resigned, the arch-Tory Timothy Pickering became Secretary of State, Oliver Wolcott headed the Treasury, and James McHenry was Secretary of War. Washington himself had become uncharacteristically partisan. "I shall not," he declared, ". . . bring a man into any office of consequence knowingly whose political tenets are adverse to the measures which the general government are pursuing; for this, in my opinion, would be a sort of political suicide."

The Antifederalist press attacked him for this policy. The President, said one newspaper, was "the scourge and misfortune of our country." Nor was Washington ever able to ignore such assaults. At a Cabinet meeting early in his administration, Jefferson recalled, Washington was visibly enraged by an attack in the press. "By god," Jefferson reports him as saying, "he had rather be on his own farm than to be made *emperor of the world*."

In September, 1796, he was ready to deliver his Farewell Address, a speech—polished by Hamilton—that would have incalculable effect on United States foreign policy for generations. Warning against the debilitating effects of sectionalism and excessive party spirit, the retiring President abjured "the insidious wiles of foreign influence." He inveighed against permanent alliances and permanent animosities, urging only "temporary alliances for extraordinary emergencies."

For himself, Washington added: "I anticipate with pleasing expectation that retreat, in which I promise myself to realize, without alloy, the sweet enjoyment of partaking, in the midst of my fellow-citizens, the benign influence of good Laws under a free Government—the ever favourite object of my heart. . . ."

Now sixty-five, the old soldier was able to go home at last. But he had put his stamp on the American Presidency forever. He had sought information "from all quarters" and judged the conflicting data "more independently than any man" John Adams "ever knew." He had, as Jefferson said, "decided the course to be pursued . . . kept the government steadily in it, unaffected by the agitation."

"It was no easy task," writes Clinton Rossiter, "to be the first occupant of a mistrusted office under a dubious Constitution." It is unmistakably true that Washington made the government of America work as only he, at his point in time, could. He built the peace on which it was based; he presided over the formulation of its legal structure; he nurtured and governed its birth. As Rossiter says, "He fulfilled the hopes of the friends of the Constitution and spiked the fears of its critics."

In retirement Washington was content "to make, and sell, a little flour. . . . To repair houses going fast to ruin. . . . To amuse myself in agriculture and rural pursuits. . . . Now and then to meet friends I esteem. . . ." But his retirement was not entirely bucolic. President Adams, alarmed by declining relations with France, named him commander of a provisional army on alert. Washington defended prosecutions under the hated and unconstitutional Alien and Sedition Acts as necessary to prevent "a disunion of the states." And he scored the Republicans for condemning every Federalist act.

But the life of the planter and landowner prevailed, as Washington began his "diurnal course with the sun." At night, he said, he felt "tired and disinclined" to write or read. Besides, he concluded, he might soon be "looking into Domesday Book."

On Saturday, December 14, 1799, the Commander in Chief, suffering from a tracheal infection (possibly tuberculosis), prepared to pay "the debt which we all must pay." "I am not afraid to go," he said. Just before he died he put the fingers of his left hand on his right wrist and counted his pulse, his lips moving.

He was buried in a vault at the foot of Mount Vernon's hill, "embalmed," said one newspaper, "by the tears of *America*."

—WILSON SULLIVAN

G. Washington

A PICTURE PORTFOLIO

This cotton handkerchief, probably made in 1777, depicts Washington as a wartime hero.

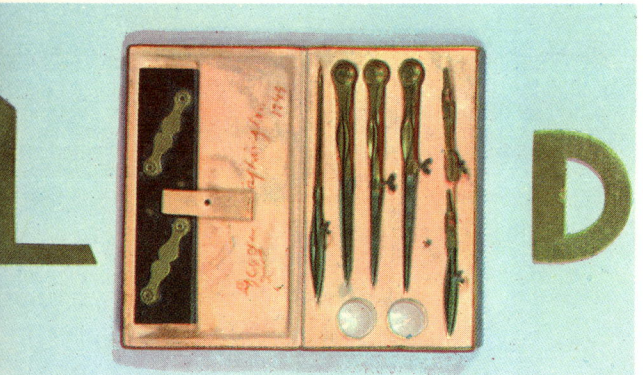

After learning the surveyor's craft with his father's tools, Washington acquired the set of drafting instruments above —probably in 1749, the date inside the case. That year he received an appointment as surveyor of Culpeper County.

On the map below, Washington sketched the land he traversed on his journey up the Ohio Valley to Fort Le Boeuf, near Lake Erie, in 1753–54. In May, 1754, he led the English troops that struck the first blow in the Seven Years' War, at a spot just northwest of the mountain spur the map shows running northward from the Allegheny Range.

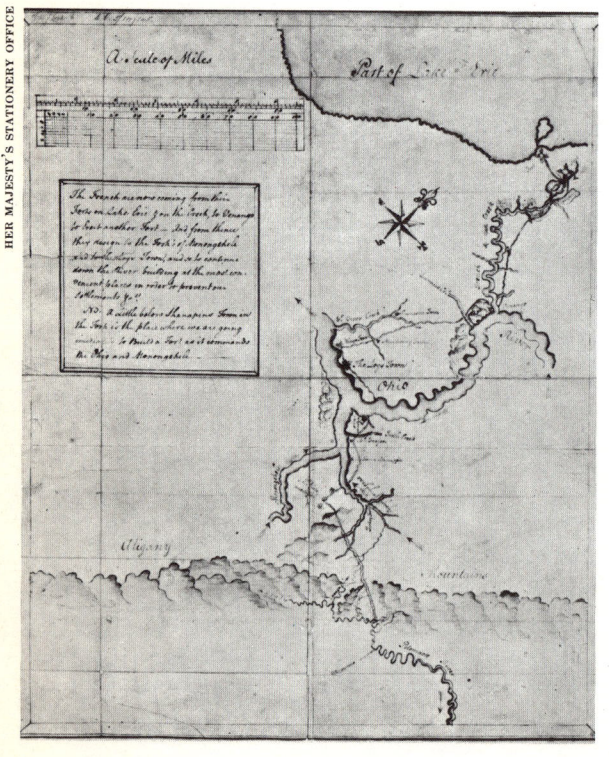

ADVENTURES OF A YOUNG VIRGINIAN

What route could the young Virginian, left without a father at eleven, take to future wealth and fame? Military service was one way. His mother said No to a proposal that George join the British navy when he was fourteen. But six years later, after he had become a surveyor and the owner of almost 1,500 acres of land, and after his beloved half brother Lawrence had died of tuberculosis, George joined the Virginia militia as a major. It was the first step on a long—and dangerous—road. Several times it seemed unlikely that he would live long enough to achieve a great future. Although he was exceptionally strong and vigorous, he suffered from malaria, smallpox, pleurisy, dysentery, and perhaps even typhoid, all before he was thirty. As a soldier, he underwent constant exposure to foul weather. On his way back from an expedition to Fort Le Boeuf in 1753, he almost drowned when he fell off his raft in the icy Allegheny River, and he was shot at (and missed) by an Indian standing less than fifty feet away. In the terrible massacre of General Braddock's troops in 1755, only a third of the officers emerged unhurt, but Washington was one of them, although four bullets had punctured his coat and two horses had been shot under him. Virginia's Governor Robert Dinwiddie, who made Washington commander in chief of the colony's militia in 1755, thought him a "braw laddie." And so he was. But he was also a lucky one.

WASHINGTON AND LEE UNIVERSITY

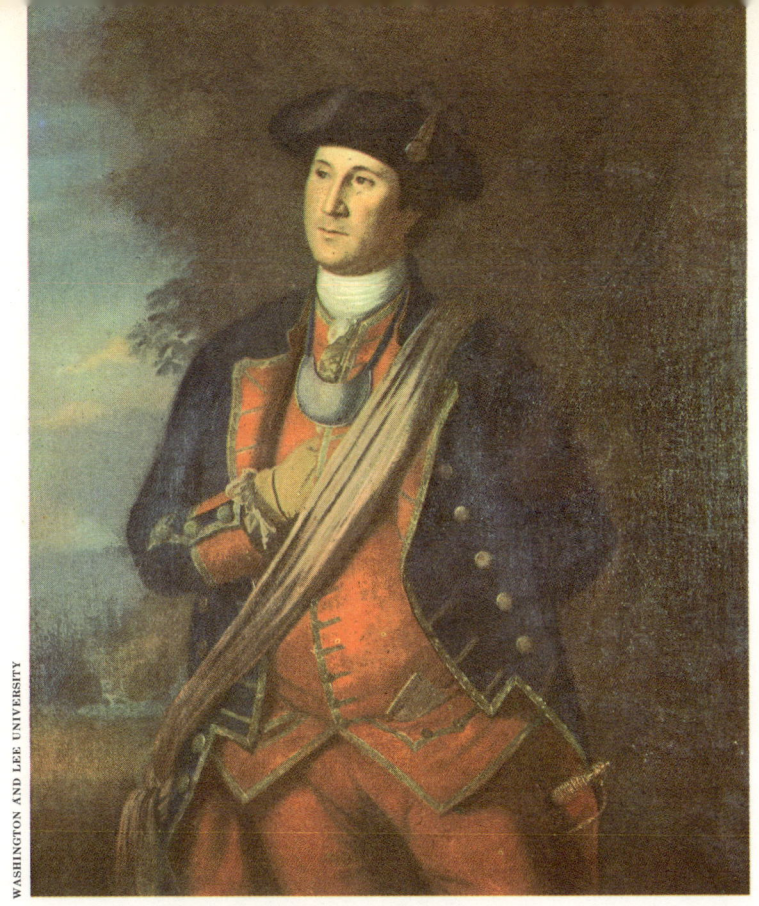

Charles Willson Peale painted the portrait of Washington at left in 1772. It is the earliest known picture of the future President, who is wearing his Virginia militia colonel's uniform. The gilt crescent-shaped gorget around his neck identifies him as an officer.

General Braddock falls from his horse, mortally hurt, while a French and Indian war party decimates his close-ranked troops, in the Edwin Willard Deming painting below of the July, 1755, Battle of the Wilderness. The figure to the right of Braddock may be Washington, his aide-de-camp. The debacle temporarily ended the English attempt to take French Fort Duquesne.

STATE HISTORICAL SOCIETY OF WISCONSIN

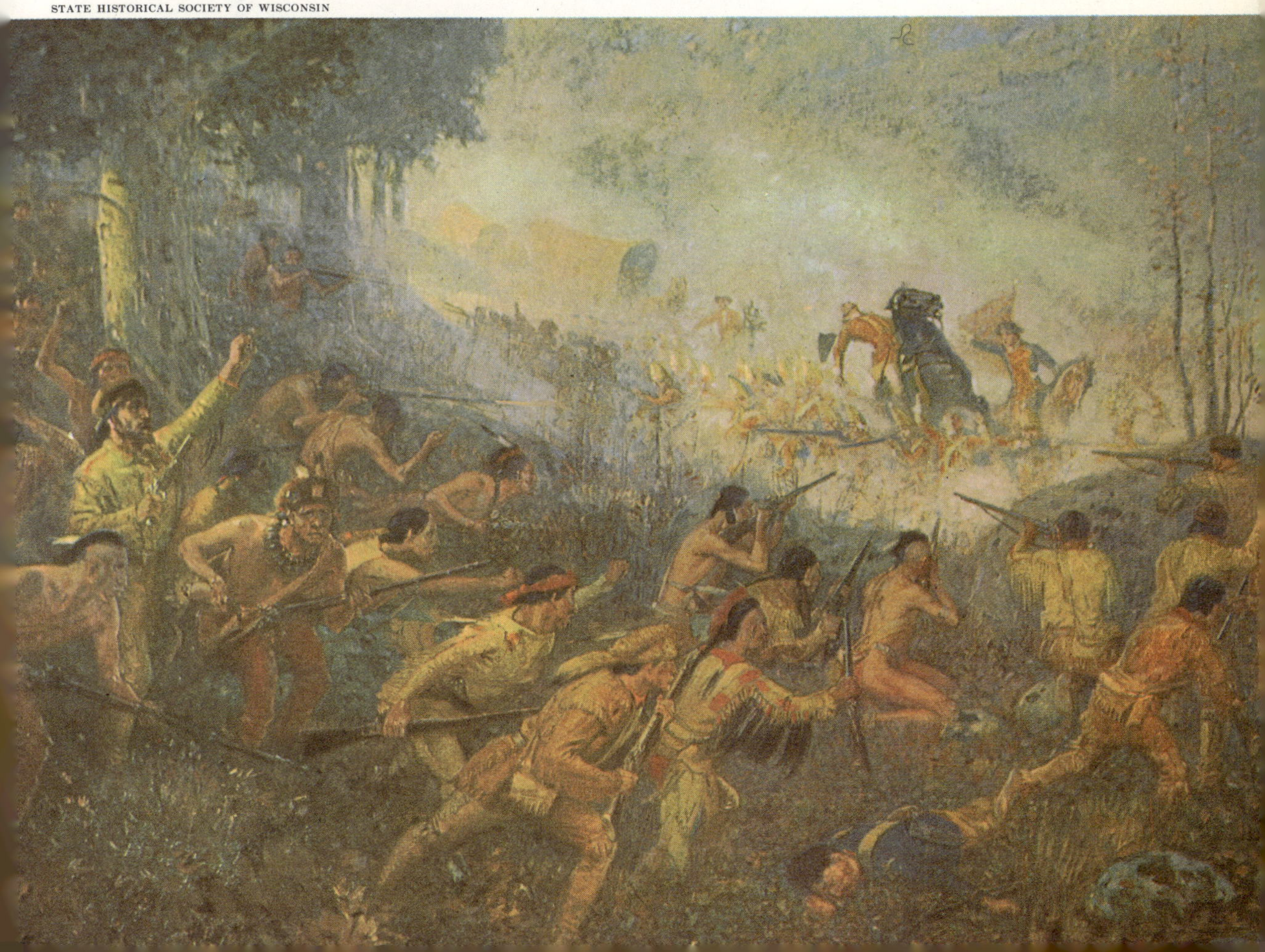

The unusual identification of the figures in this charming water color, done about 1780, suggests that the anonymous artist was a Pennsylvania German.

"SAFE HARBOR"

Charles Willson Peale painted the miniature (above) of Martha Washington, on ivory, around 1776. The General wore it in a gold locket around his neck for the rest of the war.

Below are Martha's children, John Parke (Jack) and Martha Parke (Patsy) Custis, as painted by John Wollaston.

I am now, I believe, fixed at this seat with an agreeable consort for life," Washington wrote from Mount Vernon in 1759, "and hope to find more happiness in retirement than I ever experienced amidst a wide and bustling world. . . ." Out of the Army and married to the wealthy, capable Martha Custis, Washington passed fifteen pleasant years as a more or less private man. He was chosen a member of the House of Burgesses, was made a justice of Fairfax County, and was always busy as master of Mount Vernon. But life was not without its trials and tragedies. As stepfather to his wife's two children, he agonized through the delicate Patsy Custis' five-year struggle with epilepsy and her death in 1773. The behavior of Jack Custis drove Washington to express a sarcastic wish that schooling would make Jack "fit for more useful purposes than a horse racer." A schoolmaster subsequently voiced the opinion that Jack was the most "indolent" and "surprisingly voluptuous" young man he had ever seen. But Washington was unable to bring himself to apply badly needed discipline, and Martha was a very indulgent mother. Jack lounged his way through an abbreviated education and married early. These were Washington's happiest years. Then, in 1775, his peace, and America's, were broken. "I am embarked," he wrote a few days before going to Boston as commander in chief of the Revolutionary forces, "on a wide ocean, boundless in its prospect, and in which, perhaps, no safe harbor is to be found."

COMMANDER IN CHIEF

Washington's troops forced the British to leave Boston in March, 1776, but for months afterward there was little to cheer the rebels: an expedition against Canada failed, New York fell, and Washington was chased across New Jersey in a calamitous retreat. His army finally came to rest in December on the Pennsylvania side of the Delaware River—ostensibly to defend Philadelphia, but actually, it seemed, to await the inevitable crushing blow by the British, or worse, to endure dissolution through despair, desertion, and the departure of militiamen as enlistment terms ended. Manifestly, Washington needed to kindle enthusiasm; thus, he told Congress he would go on the offensive "as soon as there shall be the least probability of doing it." He took the initiative with an advance across the Delaware on Christmas night. The battle at Trenton the following morning, in which the American soldiers killed or captured almost 1,000 Hessians, gave the rebel cause a crucial new lease on life.

Congress ordered the above medal struck to commemorate the British evacuation of Boston on March 17, 1776. It depicts Washington and members of his staff on Dorchester Heights, where the Americans, in a surprise move, had set up artillery, making untenable the British position in the city below.

As darkness fell on Christmas night, the army began its tortuous crossing of the Delaware, as shown in the painting at right by Edward Hicks. Despite high winds, freezing temperature, and thudding ice floes, the maneuver was completed before dawn.

The above painting of the Battle of Princeton is the work of Washington's stepgrandson (and Robert E. Lee's father-in-law), George Washington Parke Custis. General Hugh Mercer, kneeling at right, led the troops that made the first contact with the British and was mortally wounded by a bayonet. Washington, at left, rallied the American soldiers, overran the British position, and then chased the fleeing enemy, crying, "It is a fine fox chase, my boys."

The 9,000 soldiers who encamped at Valley Forge (right) lacked blankets, clothing, shoes, and, as the desperate proclamation seen at far right indicates, sufficient food.

OWNED BY JEREMIE ROCKWELL GARDINER

TRIUMPHS AND TRAVAILS

Washington avoided a pitched battle with a British force sent to retake Trenton; he led his army around the enemy flank in a night march and on January 3, 1777, attacked the British post at Princeton. The operation cleared most of western New Jersey of the British, but it was the last major American victory in the area for eighteen months. General Howe took Philadelphia that September, and in December, Washington's troops set up winter quarters at Valley Forge. That incredibly bitter season was profitable in one way: Baron von Steuben, a German officer, drilled the ragged rebel soldiers. The discipline paid off in June, 1778: at the Battle of Monmouth, after General Charles Lee ordered an American retreat, Washington was able to rally Lee's men from the verge of a rout and managed to hold the field against a large body of British veterans. His motley army had finally come of age.

NEW YORK PUBLIC LIBRARY

> By His Excellency
> GEORGE WASHINGTON, Esquire,
> GENERAL and COMMANDER in CHIEF of the Forces of the UNITED STATES of AMERICA.
>
> By Virtue of the Power and Direction to Me especially given, I hereby enjoin and require all Persons residing within seventy Miles of my Head Quarters to thresh one Half of their Grain by the 1st Day of February, and the other Half by the 1st Day of March next ensuing, on Pain, in Case of Failure, of having all that shall remain in Sheaves after the Period above mentioned, seized by the Commissaries and Quarter-Masters of the Army, and paid for as Straw.
>
> GIVEN under my Hand, at Head Quarters, near the Valley Forge, in Philadelphia County, this 20th Day of December, 1777.
>
> G. WASHINGTON.
>
> By His Excellency's Command,
> ROBERT H. HARRISON, Sec'y.

HISTORICAL SOCIETY OF PENNSYLVANIA
OVERLEAF: UNIVERSITY OF CALIFORNIA AT BERKELEY ART COLLECTION

Emanuel Leutze's painting shows Washington, in a fury, taking charge of the retreating troops at Monmouth.

At left, General Lee, relieved of command and stung by a dressing down from Washington, sags in his saddle.

HEROES OF THE REVOLUTION

DANIEL MORGAN

Morgan changed the course of the Revolutionary War in the South in 1781 when he won the Battle of Cowpens. A large, rough-and-tumble man, he had run away from his home near the Delaware River at eighteen and had settled in the Shenandoah Valley, where he became a teamster, farmer, and backwoods fighter. The lip scar visible in the Peale portrait above was received in an Indian ambush; a ball hit him in the neck and tore out through his face. As the American rebellion began, Congress called for "expert riflemen"; Morgan, then thirty-nine, raised a company of Virginia sharpshooters and in three weeks marched the six hundred miles to Boston. His company joined the drive to Quebec, where Morgan was captured. After an exchange of prisoners in 1776, Morgan was given command of a rifle regiment and made a colonel. He and his buckskinned troops distinguished themselves with Gates, in the North, and with Washington, near Philadelphia. Because Congress would not promote him, Morgan tried to resign in 1779, but came back to help Gates in the wake of the Camden defeat, at last becoming a brigadier general. After Cowpens, illness forced him to retire. He served his country again, notably during the Whisky Rebellion in 1794 and as a one-term congressman late in the century. Morgan died in 1802.

JOHN PAUL JONES

Born a gardener's son at Kirkbean, Scotland, in 1747, Jones went to sea at thirteen and won his first command (of a trading vessel) at twenty-one. In 1775 he was commissioned an officer in the infant American Navy and became a raider, taking prizes and threatening coastal towns on both sides of the Atlantic. Tories called him a pirate, and "the nurses of Scotland hushed their crying charges [or so Disraeli wrote] by the whisper of his name. . . ." Hot-tempered and arrogant, to his associates Jones was a difficult man. Yet his faults were outweighed by the tactical skill, single-mindedness, and bravery he displayed, as in the famous battle off Flamborough Head on September 23, 1779. In command of a motley fleet, he engaged a British convoy bound for the Baltic, and with his flagship, the ancient East Indiaman *Bonhomme Richard*, captured the bigger, better-armed *Serapis* after a long and terrible encounter that so shattered the old *Richard* it sank some thirty-six hours later. Refused flag rank due to the opposition of other officers, and bereft, in 1783, of an American Navy to serve, Jones went to Europe. In 1788, he became a rear admiral in the navy of the Russian Empress, Catherine the Great. Intrigue against him forced his retirement, however, and in 1790 he went to France, where he died two years later.

NATHANAEL GREENE

"He came to us," Henry Knox declared, "the . . . most untutored being I ever met with, but, in less than twelve months, he was equal to any General officer in the army, and very superior to most of them." A congenital limp kept Nathanael Greene from becoming a Rhode Island militia officer in 1774, but he joined as a private, and in the spring of 1775 was made commander of the troops raised to aid Massachusetts at the siege of Boston. By August, 1776, when he was thirty-three, he was a major general in the Continental Army. He fought at Trenton and Germantown, and at Valley Forge he reluctantly accepted appointment as quartermaster general. He left that job after two years because of a row with Congress. Taking charge of the war in the South in 1780, he waged a brilliant campaign of attrition against a superior force. As Greene described it, "We fight, get beat, rise and fight again." The British, cut down piecemeal while seeking the decisive battle Greene refused to give them, were compelled, by the autumn of 1781, to quit all their forts in the interior and hole up, under siege, in Charleston. Showered with honors, but physically and financially exhausted by the war, Greene was only forty-three years old when he died in 1786 on an estate that had been presented to him by a grateful state of Georgia.

GEORGE ROGERS CLARK

Child of the Virginia frontier, surveyor, and explorer, Clark was twenty-four when in 1777 he was made responsible for protecting Kentucky from British-supported Indian raids. He chose an outrageously bold course: invasion of the distant Illinois country and seizure of Detroit to stop the flow of arms. By stealth, bravery, and bluff, his band of guerrillas took the towns of Kaskaskia, Cahokia, Prairie du Rocher, and Vincennes. He won offers of peace from many Indian nations, and after Vincennes was captured by the British, he retook it. Clark never reached Detroit; control of the Old Northwest remained in armed dispute for two years after Yorktown. But at the end Clark held most of that savage theater, a fact reflected in the terms of the Treaty of Paris. He then became a commissioner of land grants and of Indian affairs. Unpaid for his military service (although Virginia gave him a sword and some land), he involved himself in unsuccessful colonizing projects in the West. He accepted a general's commission from France and would have led an attack on Spanish Louisiana, but Washington issued a proclamation against the venture. Indigent, discredited, finally a dependent cripple, Clark died near Louisville in 1818. He was the older brother of William Clark, co-leader of the famous Lewis and Clark expedition.

VICTORY AT YORKTOWN

ABOVE AND BELOW: MUSÉE DE VERSAILLES, COURTESY OF COLONIAL WILLIAMSBURG

After ravaging Virginia during the spring of 1781, Lord Cornwallis brought his troops to Yorktown to await reinforcements. Besieged there by Franco-American forces under Washington and Rochambeau, and prevented by the French navy from escaping by sea, Cornwallis realized that his situation was hopeless. The painting above, by eyewitness Louis Van Blarenberghe, shows the French marching into the siege positions; below, the surrendering redcoats parade between the French (rear) and the Americans on October 18, 1781.

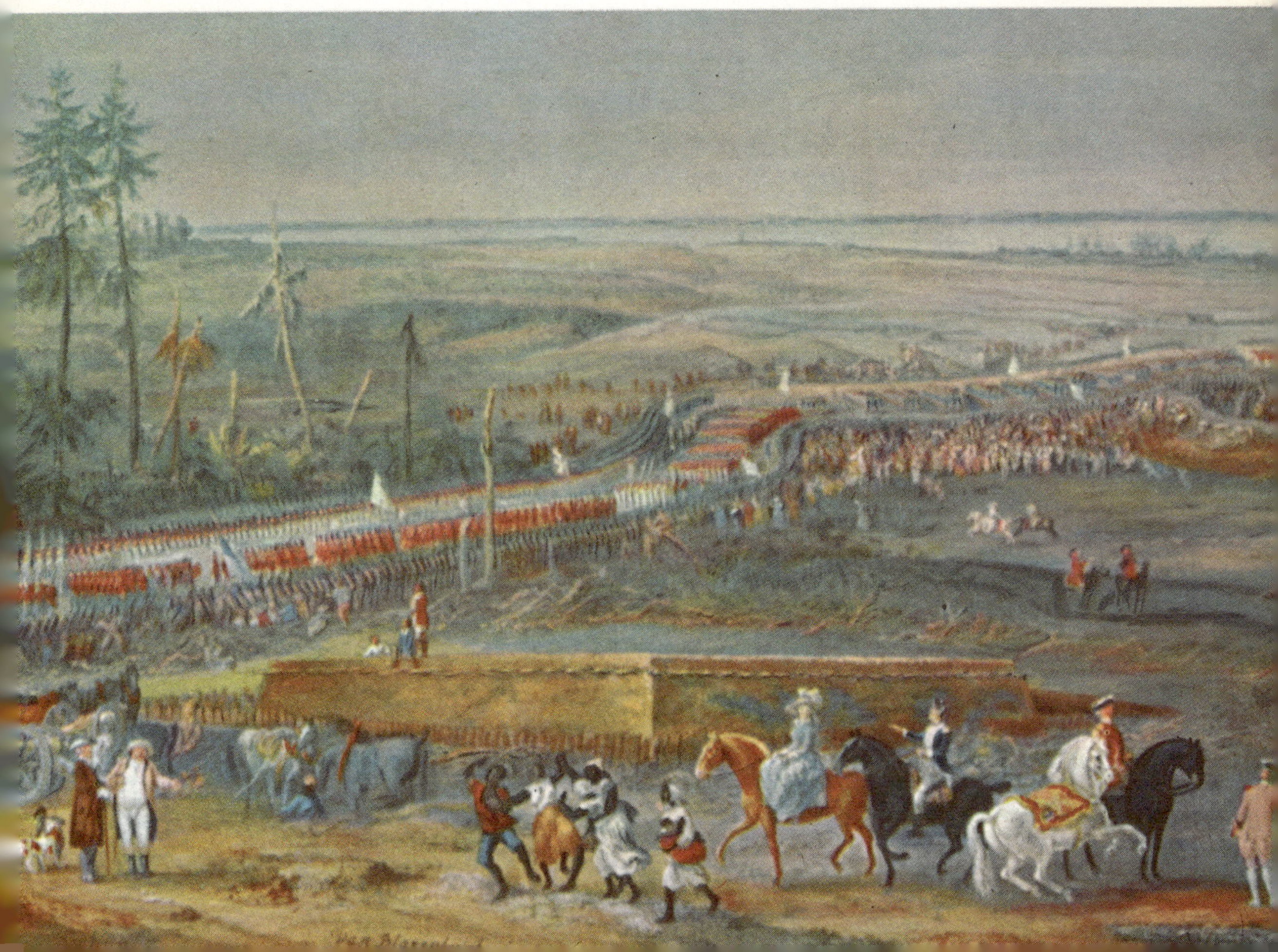

MOUNT VERNON

After the war, Washington settled into what he hoped would be permanent repose as planter and host at Mount Vernon. His estate, once known as Epsewasson, had been in the family since the seventeenth century and had been renamed Mount Vernon, after British Admiral Edward Vernon, by Washington's half brother Lawrence. After leasing the property in 1754 from his widowed sister-in-law (he inherited it when she died in 1761), the General added a second story and wings to the main house, imported furniture for it, and planted trees around it. Gradually he added to the original 2,126 acres; this growth continued until the plantation encompassed more than 8,000 acres, including five farms. Between 1783 and 1787, the banquet hall and the cupola atop the hipped roof were finished, outbuildings were added or improved, and the bowling green in front of the mansion was graded. Washington found directing these improvements and looking after the farming exceedingly satisfying, but the nation needed him, and he was called away: first to attend the Constitutional Convention in 1787, then to assume the Presidency two years later.

NATIONAL GALLERY OF ART, GIFT OF EDGAR WILLIAM AND BERNICE CHRYSLER GARBISCH

An unknown artist painted this view of the Mount Vernon mansion circa 1790. In the foreground the Washington family strolls on the bowling green. Nelly Custis, Martha's granddaughter, is at the left. Washington, with cane, and Martha walk arm in arm. The pair at the right is thought to be young George Custis and his tutor.

The high secretary below was a late addition to Washington's study. He bought it in Philadelphia as he prepared for retirement from the Presidency. The desk was willed to Dr. James Craik, a friend since 1754 and one of the attending physicians at Washington's deathbed. It was reacquired for Mount Vernon from the doctor's descendants in 1905.

The Palladian window above is considered to be one of the most striking details in the handsome New Room—the banquet hall completed in 1787. The curtains are of dimity, with green satin festoons.

An excellent sample of early Virginia architecture, the West Parlor (below) was probably finished just before Washington moved into the house with his new bride. The Washington portrait is by C. W. Peale.

THE FIRST PRESIDENT

Before he left Mount Vernon in the spring of 1789, the President-elect confessed to Henry Knox deep misgivings about his new role. He felt, he said, like a felon on the way to be hanged; he foresaw "an ocean of difficulties." His journey north was a triumph. On April 23, a week before the inaugural, he was rowed across New York Bay from Elizabethtown to the temporary federal capital at New York. Cannon boomed and thousands of citizens on the shore cheered emotionally. The city was full to overflowing; one visitor exclaimed, "We shall remain here if we have to sleep in tents as many will have to do." On April 30, the first President was sworn in on the balcony of Federal Hall. Then he retired inside to deliver his Inaugural Address. Despite the city's joy and the dignity of the occasion, Washington's extreme discomfort was evident to Senator Maclay of Pennsylvania, who noted how the President fidgeted and fumbled with his papers. And Massachusetts Congressman Fisher Ames wrote of Washington's "modesty, actually shaking; his voice deep, a little tremulous, and so low as to call for close attention. . . ." The General was right; his greatest trial had begun.

In New York Bay, Washington's triumphal barge (left), bearing federal, state, and city dignitaries, and "rowed by thirteen pilots of this harbor, dressed in white uniform," neared the landing at the foot of Wall Street, while gaily decorated ships and the cannon on the Battery fired thirteen-gun salutes. The New York Daily Advertiser *referred to the event as "animated and moving beyond description."*

Amos Doolittle made the engraving below of Washington's inauguration at Federal Hall from a drawing by eyewitness Peter Lacour. After administering the oath, Chancellor Robert R. Livingston cried out, "Long live George Washington, President of the United States!" and the spectators, clogging the roadways and the rooftops and windows of the buildings along Wall and Broad streets, echoed his words.

FEDERALIST COLOSSUS

He was a revolutionary who considered the frame of the government he revolted against "the best in the world"; he was admired as a political philosopher—the brilliant advocate of strong central rule—and hated as the high-handed, egocentric party boss, even by many who shared his political beliefs.

This was Alexander Hamilton—next to the President, the dominant figure of Washington's administration. Born of a common-law marriage in the Caribbean in 1755 or 1757, Hamilton came to New York in 1772 for an education. At King's College (later Columbia), he became a leader of the unrest that led to the Revolution. While serving as an officer under Washington, he began to develop his theories of democratic rule and to campaign for a convention to enlarge the powers of the federal government. To survive, Hamilton thought, the nation would have to be what it was not under the Articles of Confederation—firmly united, with the separatist tendencies of the states kept in check, able to defend itself against attack, and dependable in economic matters. Hamilton favored government support of American commerce and the encouragement of an educated, well-to-do ruling class, whose interests would be closely tied to interests of the nation.

Many of his aristocratic ideas, drawn from the British model, clashed with strong republican feelings in the states. His plan for government did not attract support at the Constitutional Convention in 1787, and at the end of that long conclave he admitted (according to Madison) that "No man's ideas were more remote [from the final draft of the Constitution] than his own were known to be." Even so, he had been a member of the Committee of Style that produced the finished document; he pleaded for its unanimous approval by the delegates, and then went home to begin writing, with the help of Madison and Jay, arguments in favor of ratification—*The Federalist* papers. He believed that the new Constitution, imperfect though it might be, offered a viable alternative to the "anarchy and convulsion" he saw rapidly engulfing the Confederation.

Appointed Secretary of the Treasury by Washington in 1789, he continued to strengthen the federal powers. At his insistence the United States assumed full responsibility for its Revolutionary debts, and for the war debts of the states. This served to unite the wealthy creditor class behind the central government and stabilize the economy. With an excise on whisky, he confirmed the government's right to tax. Perhaps most important, his arguments in favor of the creation of a national bank—the doctrine of implied powers—gave the Constitution the flexibility it would need to cope with the changing demands of passing decades.

Hamilton was, as Thomas Jefferson once said, "a colossus" to the Federalist party. He was more, however: he was a colossus in the history of democratic government.

This portrait of Hamilton is by John Trumbull.

WASHINGTON'S APPOINTEES

JOHN JAY

First Chief Justice of the Supreme Court, the cultured and diligent Jay—born in New York City in 1745—was a noted lawyer and a member of both Continental Congresses. He served as minister to Spain from 1780 to 1782, and then participated in the peace talks in Paris. His insistence that the American commissioners be regarded as representatives of the United States, not of the "Colonies," delayed the negotiations and may have cost the United States possession of Canada, which the British might have been willing to cede in exchange for an early end to the war. Jay also shared responsibility with John Adams for suing for peace without consultation with France. The final treaty was signed in September, 1783, and Jay returned home early the next year to serve as secretary of foreign affairs. An advocate of a strong central government, he wrote five *Federalist* papers. He was named Chief Justice by Washington, but went to England in 1794 to cope with the threat of a new war. His success was limited, for the treaty bearing his name did not include British recognition of American neutrality rights. He returned to New York to find himself elected governor, and held that office for six years, retiring to private life at the age of fifty-five. Twenty-eight years later, Jay died in Bedford, New York.

JAMES WILSON

A university-educated Scot, James Wilson arrived in the colonies in 1765, at the age of twenty-three. He was soon appointed Latin tutor at the College of Philadelphia, and began studying law. By 1774, he had a large practice in southern Pennsylvania. Elected to Congress in 1775, 1782, and 1785, he signed the Declaration of Independence and spoke as a strong nationalist. In his political philosophy there was also a strain of democratic theory, but he made enemies among the rights-of-man idealists when he opposed the democratic Pennsylvania constitution of 1776. His philosophy and debating skills influenced the federal Constitution in 1787; among his contributions to the convention was an able exposition of the theory of divided (federal-state) sovereignty. He asked Washington for the job of Chief Justice in the new government, but was made an associate justice instead. On the bench and in law lectures, he promulgated his Federalist ideas further, trying to establish himself as an American Blackstone. He did not quite achieve that eminence, partly because he had become deeply involved in land speculation and was caught short by a recession in the 1790's; hounded by creditors, he began to fall apart emotionally. Wilson contracted malaria in 1798 and died that same year in an inn at Edenton, North Carolina.

HENRY KNOX

There was, wrote Washington, "no one whom I have loved more sincerely" than General Knox. Seventh of his Scotch-Irish parents' ten sons, Knox was born in Boston in 1750, quit school early to support his widowed mother, and celebrated coming of age by opening The London Book-Store in Boston in 1771. A soldier while still in his teens, he rose rapidly in rank during the Revolution, becoming Washington's artillery commander in 1775 and brigadier general the following year. He hauled cannon over the mountains from Fort Ticonderoga to Dorchester Heights, forcing the British to evacuate Boston. He fought in the battles around New York and in the surprise attack on Trenton, and gave Washington dependable support in numerous other engagements, including Yorktown. A major general by 1781, Knox commanded the Army post at West Point, where soon the military academy he had suggested would be founded. He was named Secretary of War in 1785, and retained the position under Washington, unsuccessfully urging the construction of a strong military establishment. Huge, energetic, self-confident, he "retired" in 1794 and began a many-sided business and political career, mostly in Maine. A chicken bone, stuck in his intestinal tract, ended General Knox's life in 1806.

EDMUND RANDOLPH

Scion of a leading Virginia family, Randolph studied at William and Mary and in his father's law office before commencing a remarkably rapid rise to national prominence. An aide-de-camp to Washington during the Revolution, he became attorney general of his state at twenty-three. He was elected to the Continental Congress three years later, in 1779, and to the governorship of Virginia in 1786. As a delegate to the Constitutional Convention, he presented the Virginia Plan —the foundation of the finished Constitution. But he opposed a one-man executive branch, criticized the breadth of power given the central government by the Constitution, and refused to sign that document in Philadelphia. In the crucial Virginia Ratification Convention, however, he supported adoption of the document as the practical course. Washington made him Attorney General and, after Jefferson resigned, Secretary of State. Randolph served capably in that difficult post until the summer of 1795; then rumors (the accuracy of which is still in doubt) of corrupt dealings with a French diplomat resulted in Randolph's resignation. He returned to his private law practice and, in 1807, led the successful defense of former Vice President Aaron Burr at his trial for treason. Edmund Randolph was sixty years old when he died in 1813.

The unpopular exciseman, confiscating tax evaders' whisky, comes to a bad end in this antifederal cartoon.

THE WHISKY REBELLION

Washington considered the development of a firm national government, based on the new Constitution, his prime responsibility as President. The most crucial test of federal strength—and one of the most important events of his administration—came in 1794. In western Pennsylvania, an organized rebellion broke out over the federal excise tax on whisky. Responding to the crisis, President Washington affirmed the taxation powers of Congress and the legitimacy of executive and judicial responsibility for enforcing the laws. "If the laws are to be so trampled upon with impunity," he warned, "and a minority . . . is to dictate to the majority, there is an end put, at one stroke, to republican government." To assure that the uprising would be controlled before it became a general Antifederalist conflagration, Washington called for the enlistment of an army, and he and Secretary of the Treasury Alexander Hamilton rode with the 12,000-man force as it marched off toward insurrectionist territory. This display of executive determination brought to an end the Whisky Rebellion without one shot having to be fired.

The few "Whisky Boys" who were caught in the federal army's sweep through western Pennsylvania were allowed to sign the oath at right, and to go free. Two were imprisoned, but they were later pardoned by Washington.

In the painting below by eyewitness Frederick Kemmelmeyer, Washington actively assumes his presidential role as Commander in Chief of the armed forces, reviewing some of the troops raised against the whisky rebels.

In this family portrait by Edward Savage, two of Martha's grandchildren, George Washington Parke Custis and Eleanor Parke Custis, join the Washingtons around a table spread with a map of the Potomac River. Martha points to the site of the federal capital, under construction when Washington died.

Attended by his wife, three physicians, and members of his household, Washington died quietly the night of December 14, 1799. "With perfect resignation and a full possession of his reason," wrote his secretary, Tobias Lear, "he closed his well spent life."

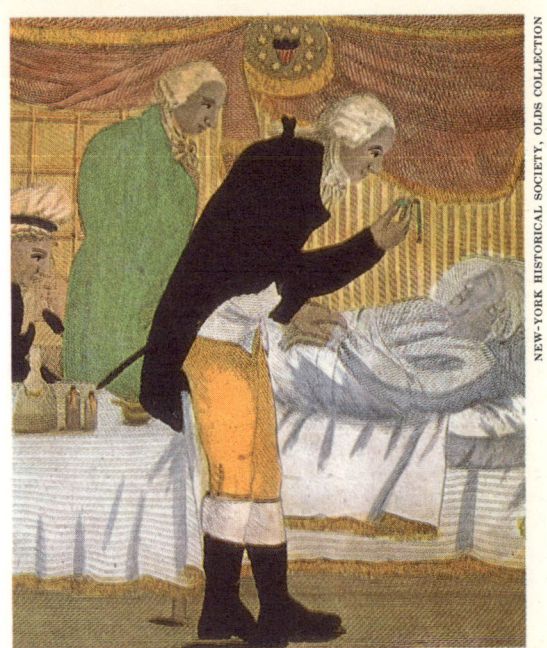

"THE WEARIED TRAVELLER"

To the wearied traveller, who sees a resting-place, and is bending his body to lean thereon, I now compare myself," Washington wrote, with poetic poignancy, on his next-to-last day as President. "The remainder of my life . . . will be occupied in rural amusement." He predicted he would not stir more than twenty miles from Mount Vernon the rest of his days. But complete withdrawal was neither his style, nor his lot; John Adams' troubles, the war crisis of 1798, and the building of the nearby federal city all engaged his energies from time to time. Even so, he devoted long hours to the running of his plantation, played host to numerous guests, enjoyed the company of the chatty, cheery Martha, and indulged himself by letting his correspondence slide a bit. Though he had jokingly "entered into an engagement" with friends "not to quitt the theatre of this world" before the turn of the new century (so Martha wrote), Washington signed his will in July, 1799, and died in December of that year, defaulting on his "contract" by just eighteen days.

C. W. Peale painted him during the Revolutionary War.

Joseph Wright portrayed General Washington in 1784.

Adams thought this Savage portrait was the best.

This painting by A. V. Wertmuller was done in 1794.

A MAN OF MANY FACES

The first President was one of the most frequently painted, drawn, and sculpted men of his time. "*In for a penny, in for a pound*, is an old adage," he remarked amusedly in 1785. "I am so hackneyed to the touches of the painter's pencil, that I am *now* altogether at their beck; and sit, 'like Patience on a monument,' whilst they are delineating the lines of my face. It is a proof, among many others, of what habit and custom can accomplish. At first I was as impatient at the request, and as restive under the operation, as a colt is of the saddle. The next time I submitted very reluctantly, but with less flouncing. Now, no dray-horse moves more readily to his thill than I to the painter's chair." Some of the portraits reveal, in the set of his jaw, Washington's chronic problems with false teeth; most fail to show the President's true complexion—sallow, scarred, and pock-marked. But from most of the numerous attempts to portray him—even though they are so various it is sometimes hard to believe they are all paintings of the same man—there emanates a sense of dignity, of seriousness bordering on sadness, and of the artists' consciousness of their subject as a hero.

The above sketch, by Benjamin Latrobe, is reputed to have been drawn at the Mount Vernon dinner table.

Jean Antoine Houdon, the French sculptor, came to the United States in 1785 and made the life mask below for a bust of Washington. Experts point out that pressure of the plaster sometimes reshapes the face, making such a mask an inexact impression.

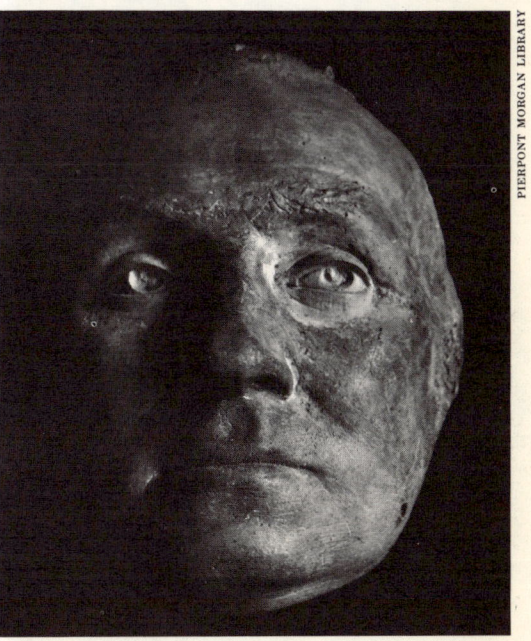

MONUMENT TO A HERO

Almost 556 feet tall, the Washington Monument towers over the spacious Capital city, its white marble facing tinted by the changing light of day, glowing under floodlights at night, and echoed in the long reflecting pool. The idea of a national memorial to Washington was conceived in 1833, and the design was more or less settled on in 1836, but the cornerstone was not laid until Independence Day, 1848, and by 1858 only 156 feet of obelisk had been erected. No work at all was done on it for the next twenty years—a period of turmoil for the nation. Construction began again in 1878, and six years later, on a blustery December day, the monument was finally finished.

In the 1875 cartoon above, the spirit of Washington chides Columbia for failing to finish his monument.

The exotic design at left was entered in the Washington National Monument Society's contest.

The winner of that competition, opposite, was the work of Robert Mills. The Monument Society then eliminated the neoclassic temple base, with its heroic sculpture of Washington in a war chariot. Even so, the monument cost $1,187,710 to build.

FACTS IN SUMMARY: GEORGE WASHINGTON

CHRONOLOGY

UNITED STATES		WASHINGTON
	1732	Born February 11 (February 22, n.s.)
	1748	Joins surveying expedition to Shenandoah
	1749	Appointed county surveyor
	1751	Visits Barbados
	1752	Lawrence Washington dies
		Receives commission in Virginia militia
	1753	Delivers ultimatum to French at Fort Le Boeuf
French and Indian War begins	1754	Attacks French party near Fort Duquesne
		Capitulates at Fort Necessity
	1755	Serves as aide to General Braddock
		Appointed commander in chief of militia
French abandon Ohio Valley	1758	Elected to House of Burgesses
		Resigns commission
	1759	Marries Martha Custis
	1761	Inherits Mount Vernon
Treaty of Paris	1763	
Stamp Act	1765	
Townshend Acts	1767	
Massachusetts Circular Letter	1768	Becomes a justice of Fairfax County
House of Burgesses dissolved	1769	
Boston Massacre	1770	Secures Ohio Valley lands for veterans of French and Indian War
Boston Tea Party	1773	
Intolerable Acts	1774	Delegate to First Continental Congress
First Continental Congress		
Lexington and Concord	1775	Delegate to Second Continental Congress
Bunker Hill		
Second Continental Congress		Elected commander in chief of Army
British evacuate Boston	1776	Siege of Boston
Declaration of Independence		Loses N.Y. in battles of Long Island and White Plains
		Retreats through N.J.
		Takes Trenton
Burgoyne surrenders at Saratoga	1777	Takes Princeton
		Defeated at Brandywine and Germantown
Articles of Confederation adopted		Winters at Valley Forge
		Conway Cabal exposed
Franco-American alliance	1778	Wins Battle of Monmouth
Spain enters war	1779	
British take Charleston	1780	
Articles of Confederation ratified	1781	Receives surrender of Cornwallis at Yorktown
Treaty of Paris	1783	Bids farewell to officers
		Resigns commission
Constitutional Convention	1787	Elected president of Constitutional Convention
Constitution ratified	1788	
French Revolution	1789	Elected President
Bill of Rights		
Capital moved to Philadelphia	1790	Signs assumption bill
Emergence of rival parties		
District of Columbia established	1791	Signs National Bank charter
		Approves excise tax
	1792	Re-elected President
Jefferson resigns as Secretary of State	1793	Issues Neutrality Proclamation
		Demands recall of Genêt
Jay's Treaty signed in London	1794	Suppresses Whisky Rebellion

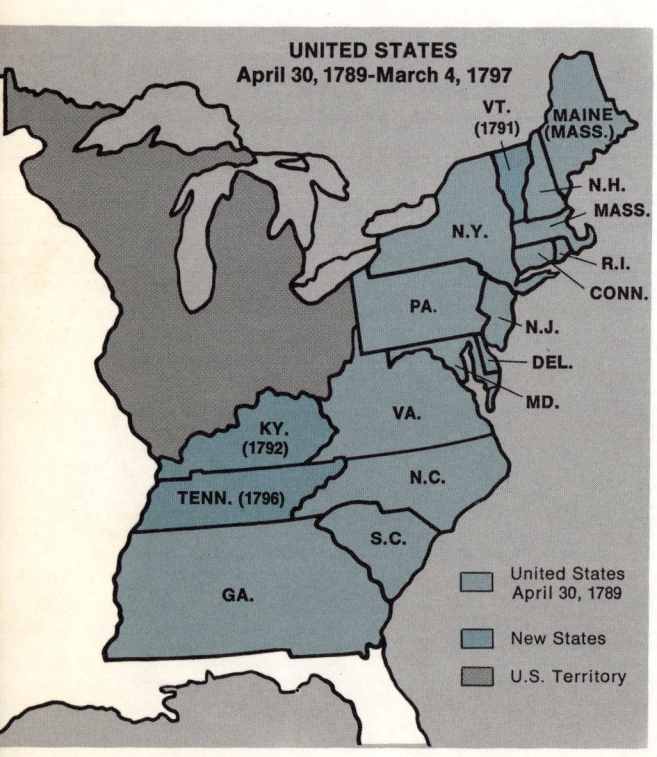

UNITED STATES
April 30, 1789–March 4, 1797

- United States April 30, 1789
- New States
- U.S. Territory

Hamilton resigns from Cabinet	1795	*Reorganizes Cabinet*
Pinckney's Treaty signed in Madrid		
John Adams elected President	1796	*Publishes Farewell Address*
	1797	*Retires to Mount Vernon*
Undeclared naval war with France	1798	*Appointed commander of provisional army*
	1799	*Dies December 14*

BIOGRAPHICAL FACTS

BIRTH: Pope's Creek (Wakefield), Westmoreland County, Va., Feb. 11, 1732 (Feb. 22, new style)
ANCESTRY: English
FATHER: Augustine Washington; b. Westmoreland County, Va., 1694; d. King George County, Va., April 12, 1743
FATHER'S OCCUPATION: Planter
MOTHER: Mary Ball Washington; b. Lancaster County, Va., 1708; d. near Fredericksburg, Va., Aug. 25, 1789
BROTHERS: Samuel (1734–1781); John Augustine (1736–1787); Charles (1738–1799)
SISTERS: Elizabeth (1733–1797); Mildred (1739–1740)
HALF BROTHERS: Lawrence (1718–1752); Augustine (1720–1735)
HALF SISTER: Jane (1722–1735)
WIFE: Martha Dandridge Custis; b. New Kent County, Va., June 21, 1731; d. Mount Vernon, Va., May 22, 1802
MARRIAGE: Kent County, Va., Jan. 6, 1759
CHILDREN: None (adopted two children from his wife's first marriage)
HOME: Mount Vernon, Va.
EDUCATION: Private tutoring by family
RELIGIOUS AFFILIATION: Episcopalian
OCCUPATIONS BEFORE PRESIDENCY: Surveyor; soldier; planter
MILITARY SERVICE: Virginia militia (1752–1758); commander in chief of Continental Army (1775–1783)
PRE-PRESIDENTIAL OFFICES: Member of Virginia House of Burgesses; Justice of Fairfax County; Delegate to First and Second Continental Congresses; President of Constitutional Convention
POLITICAL PARTY: Favored Federalists
AGE AT INAUGURATION: 57
OCCUPATION AFTER PRESIDENCY: Planter
DEATH: Mount Vernon, Va., Dec. 14, 1799
PLACE OF BURIAL: Mount Vernon, Va.

ELECTION OF 1789

(In 1789 and 1792, each elector voted for two men.)

CANDIDATES	ELECTORAL VOTE
George Washington	69
John Adams	34
John Jay	9
Nine others	26

FIRST ADMINISTRATION

INAUGURATION: April 30, 1789; Federal Hall, New York City
VICE PRESIDENT: John Adams
SECRETARY OF STATE: Thomas Jefferson
SECRETARY OF THE TREASURY: Alexander Hamilton
SECRETARY OF WAR: Henry Knox
ATTORNEY GENERAL: Edmund Randolph
POSTMASTER GENERAL: Samuel Osgood; Timothy Pickering (from Aug. 19, 1791)
SUPREME COURT APPOINTMENTS: John Jay, Chief Justice (1789); John Rutledge (1789); William Cushing (1789); Robert H. Harrison (1789); James Wilson (1789); John Blair (1789); James Iredell (1790); Thomas Johnson (1791)
FIRST CONGRESS (March 4, 1789–March 4, 1791):
Senate: 17 Federalists; 9 Antifederalists
House: 38 Federalists; 26 Antifederalists
SECOND CONGRESS (March 4, 1791–March 4, 1793):
Senate: 16 Federalists; 13 Democratic-Republicans
House: 37 Federalists; 33 Democratic-Republicans
STATES ADMITTED: Vermont (1791); Kentucky (1792)

ELECTION OF 1792

CANDIDATES	ELECTORAL VOTE
George Washington	132
John Adams	77
George Clinton	50
Two others	5

SECOND ADMINISTRATION

INAUGURATION: March 4, 1793; Federal Hall, Philadelphia
VICE PRESIDENT: John Adams
SECRETARY OF STATE: Thomas Jefferson; Edmund Randolph (from Jan. 2, 1794); Timothy Pickering (from Aug. 20, 1795)
SECRETARY OF THE TREASURY: Alexander Hamilton; Oliver Wolcott, Jr. (from Feb. 2, 1795)
SECRETARY OF WAR: Henry Knox; Timothy Pickering (from Jan. 2, 1795); James McHenry (from Feb. 6, 1796)
ATTORNEY GENERAL: Edmund Randolph; William Bradford (from Jan. 29, 1794); Charles Lee (from Dec. 10, 1795)
POSTMASTER GENERAL: Timothy Pickering; Joseph Habersham (from Feb. 25, 1795)
SUPREME COURT APPOINTMENTS: William Paterson (1793); John Rutledge, Chief Justice (1795); Samuel Chase (1796); Oliver Ellsworth, Chief Justice (1796)
THIRD CONGRESS (March 4, 1793–March 4, 1795):
Senate: 17 Federalists; 13 Democratic-Republicans
House: 57 Democratic-Republicans; 48 Federalists
FOURTH CONGRESS (March 4, 1795–March 4, 1797):
Senate: 19 Federalists; 13 Democratic-Republicans
House: 54 Federalists; 52 Democratic-Republicans
STATE ADMITTED: Tennessee (1796)

THE SECOND PRESIDENT (1797–1801)

JOHN ADAMS

John Adams was not born into the First Family of America; he founded it. Although his Puritan ancestors were active in local affairs, the Adamses of Massachusetts remained typical colonial farmers until John and Susanna Boylston Adams of Braintree parish had their first son. In this Adams, born on October 19, 1735, there developed a brilliance of intellect and a uniqueness of character that he passed to his sons and they to theirs. But if character separated John Adams from his forefathers and distinguished his descendants, it also forbade rapport between the Adamses and the American people, to whose service they were totally devoted.

That John Adams became President at all is one more tribute to the Founding Fathers of the United States: it is doubtful that he could progress very far in modern politics. Early in his career, when he began to devote himself to the cause of American independence, he maintained a legalistic posture high above the issues in which his fellow patriots were emotionally involved. He was haughty, condescending, self-righteous, cantankerous, throughout his life; he was so aloof that even the people with whom he joined forces were not always sure he was on their side. Yet they were delighted when he was, for he was incorruptible and extraordinarily intelligent, and he had the courage to stand by his convictions at any cost. Another facet of the prismatic Adams character was introspectiveness. He could be unusually objective about himself: the self-portraiture in his diary might have been written by a disinterested party. He called himself "puffy, vain, conceited." He wrote that vanity was his "cardinal folly," and often his contemporaries paid tribute to his perceptiveness by agreeing with him.

While his offspring appear to have been born with the Adams character, John Adams had to develop it. In his youth he much preferred farm chores

John Adams in 1798, painted by William Winstanley

Paul Revere made this engraving of Harvard in 1767, twelve years after Adams' graduation from college.

to schoolwork, and he studied agriculture (which remained his hobby for life) more than Latin. But his parents had provided a model for him: his uncle Joseph Adams, a Harvard graduate who had been a schoolmaster and then a clergyman of some stature. Thus in 1751, at the age of sixteen, Adams entered Harvard. There, two years later, he began his diary. To our knowledge, no earlier Adams had worked out his ideas in writing, but John felt a need to do so. As historian James Truslow Adams (no relation) put it, "that insatiable desire to write, write, write" entered the Adams genes and became a hereditary compulsion.

After graduating from Harvard, Adams was employed as master of the grammar school in Worcester, Massachusetts. From the start, teaching was at best barely tolerable for him. Adams was at that time soft-spoken and introverted, almost shy. The boys—there were fifty of them in his class, ranging in age from five to fifteen—at first behaved with some restraint, testing him, making certain that a wolf was not hidden beneath the sheepskin. Before long the pupils had the measure of their master and took the upper hand. They were to Adams "little runtlings, just capable of lisping A, B, C, and troubling the master"; the classroom became for him a "school of affliction." Yet the apparent alternative, the ministry, seemed no less depressing. Adams was bathed in gloom until the summer of 1756, when he began finding nightly retreat in the law offices of James Putnam. Two years later he left teaching, passed the bar examination, and began practicing law at Braintree.

In order to observe the methods of more experienced lawyers, Adams attended trials throughout the surrounding counties. One of the attorneys he greatly admired was fiery James Otis of Boston, advocate general of the vice admiralty. When, early in 1761, Otis resigned his court-appointed office to argue the colonial case against the Writs of Assistance before the chief justice of Massachusetts, Adams attended the hearing.

The Writs of Assistance were legal permits giving inspectors the right to enter and search any ship, warehouse, or private home where smuggled goods were thought to be hidden. Although colonial courts had long been empowered to issue writs, it had not often been necessary or prudent to do so. After the Seven Years' War, however, Parliament found itself in debt while colonial prosperity had never been healthier, especially in Massachusetts, and the courts were ordered to issue writs. It was difficult enough to suddenly enforce a long-ignored law, but to complicate matters further for England, King George II died. Traditionally, all writs automatically expired six months after the death of a monarch, and according to Otis the English decision not to withdraw the writs was in opposition to British law. Moreover, Otis added emotionally, enforcement of the writs was a violation of an Englishman's established right to freedom from intrusion in his own home.

Sixty years later John Adams would write that in the council chamber where Otis spoke "the child Independence was born." Adams' diary of the time makes only passing mention of the speech, but retrospective drama was characteristic of Adams' writing.

Beneath the cold, intellectual façade, under the detachment and pomposity, was a John Adams who was more romantic than he ever would have admitted. He could be quite sentimental, and he felt with incredible depth. He fell in and out of love as often as a schoolgirl. He cherished the ladies and pampered them and left them untouched—by him anyway—on their pedestals. An early sweetheart, Hannah Quincy, tempered her affection for him because she thought no ordinary woman could ever return the immeasurable quantity of love that John Adams had in him to give. On his part Adams longed for a wife and family, but he was cautious, and he proposed marriage only once—to Abigail Smith. They were married in 1764.

Hannah Quincy had been right: Abigail Smith Adams was no ordinary woman. She read more than a lady was supposed to; she was smarter than a woman ought to have been; and she spoke out when convention called for feminine silence. She was the perfect wife for Adams, for she managed to keep the cold, impersonal statesman out of the home and the devoted, at times even tender, family man in. She humored his hypochondria and made light of his constant premonitions of early death. Adams did not emerge as a public figure until after his marriage. True, the national issues were growing in intensity, but he still had elements of the timid schoolmaster in him. Now they disappeared, replaced by a directness—sometimes even a flair—that suited the role he was about to play.

For one thing, he began to spend more time with his cousin Samuel. Sam Adams, bankrupt businessman, radical, patriot, scholar, teacher, rabble-rouser—depending on who was describing him—was in 1764 the Boston tax collector who opposed the taxes he was supposed to collect. Thirteen years older than John, Sam had the vision to look beyond the superficiality of individual issues to the larger issues that were dividing Crown and colonies. Although John Adams would remain considerably more cautious than his cousin, he too began to view each issue as part of the whole.

The Stamp Act of 1765 provides a case in point. The surface issue was censorship: because the act would require the colonials to purchase stamps for every printed document, from wills to playing cards, from insurance policies to newspapers, the Crown would have the opportunity to refuse to sell stamps for material it regarded as unfavorable. But the real issue, just as it had been with the Writs of Assistance, was taxation without representation, and that—so the saying was beginning to go—was tyranny. When word came that the act had been passed, angered colonials swung into action. The militant Sons of Liberty stormed and wrecked the home of Massachusetts-born Lieutenant Governor Thomas Hutchinson, and Sam Adams organized a blockade of the custom house to prevent the stamps from being distributed. John Adams wrote a series of brilliant articles for the Boston *Gazette*, condemning the act purely on legal grounds, turning for premises to British law, claiming that it was "inconsistent with the spirit of the common law and of the essential fundamental principles of the British constitution that we should be subject to any tax imposed by the British Parliament; because we are not represented in that assembly in any sense. . . ." When a Massachusetts General Court was called for October,

The bland entries in John Adams' diary, right, bespeak the tedium of his teaching days in Worcester.

© 1966 MASS. HIST. SOC., BY PERMISSION OF THE BELKNAP PRESS OF HARVARD UNIVERSITY PRESS

he wrote a list of recommendations for the Braintree delegate. To his surprise, forty towns in Massachusetts adopted as their own his Braintree Instructions, which made John Adams a figure of importance.

Of the actions of the Sons of Liberty he was extremely critical. To oppose an unjust law in court, to petition, to call a congress—these were legal rights; but to react with vigilante vandalism was not. Such was John Adams' position until the courts were suddenly closed. The government's reasoning was clear enough: all legal documents had to be stamped; the colonials would not permit distribution of the stamps; therefore the business of the law could no longer proceed. Shaken from his perch, Adams saw the weakness in his commitment to legality. How does one employ legal channels when the channels are closed? Even after the Stamp Act was repealed and the courts reopened, Adams was troubled: the Crown had closed the courts once, and could do so again.

Although he remained a moderate, favoring legal petition as the first weapon of protest, Adams no longer equated forceful resistance with treason. He grew closer to Sam Adams and James Otis, and when he refused the governor's appointment to the lucrative post of advocate general of the admiralty, he was acknowledged by the people of Boston as a patriot, albeit a stuffy one.

But Adams placed his political career on the block before it even got going. On March 5, 1770, a squad of soldiers under the command of Captain Thomas Preston paraded past a crowd of Bostonians. During the customary exchange of insults, the crowd became a mob; stones were thrown, shots were fired, five civilians were killed and several injured. When no other lawyer would agree to defend the soldiers involved in the Boston Massacre, the objective John Adams announced that he would be the defense attorney. Before the trial began, Adams was persuaded to become a candidate for the provincial legislature. Having no confidence in the judgment of the people, he was sure that the defender of British soldiers could not possibly win; but he entered the race anyway and, much to his surprise, won by the considerable ratio of 4 to 1.

Though the people who elected him admired his courage in standing forward for the defendants, they were not prepared for Adams' success in court. Preston was acquitted, two of the soldiers were convicted of minor infractions and given light sentences, and the rest were exonerated. Adams was ostracized: the Sons of Liberty called

The print below depicts the "Indians" at the height of the Boston Tea Party. Although he did not participate, John Adams called the event "magnificent."

him a deserter, the patriot press turned against him, and, perhaps most painful of all, Sam Adams wrote a series of articles signed VINDEX, which implied collusion between defense and royalist court. To make matters worse, the royalists began wooing John Adams, assuming that he had come over to their side. The sensitivity he was usually capable of controlling asserted itself: he packed up and went back to Braintree. "Farewell politics," he wrote in his diary.

He kept to his farewell for two and a half years. Then, late in 1772, Parliament introduced reforms to provincial courts. Some letters by Thomas Hutchinson, which proved that the courts had been rigged previously and that the new "reforms" were calculated to make the courts entirely subordinate to the Crown, were intercepted by Benjamin Franklin and sent to Sam Adams, who published them. On January 4, 1773, the first of a series of eight long articles decrying the situation appeared in the *Gazette* over the signature of John Adams. In May the legislature nominated him to sit in the upper chamber of the House of Representatives; and when the governor vetoed his name, Adams was returned to patriot graces.

In the autumn of 1773, the much-scarred umbilical cord between Crown and colonies was stretched to the breaking point. Three years earlier, Parliament had repealed most of the duties on colonial imports imposed by the Townshend Acts but had left the tax on tea. The colonists had evaded the tax by smuggling tea from the Netherlands, while tea leaves were rotting in London warehouses. But now the East India Company, heavily indebted to the government, was nearly bankrupt, and Parliament awarded it exclusive right to the sale of tea in the American colonies. This was the last straw for the colonials; they would not have their economy ruined by monopolies. On the evening of December 16, 1773, the merchant ship *Dartmouth*, first of three tea-bearing vessels to dock in Boston Harbor, was the site of a masquerade fete attended by a group of Indian-guised Bostonians, who summarily tossed the cargo overboard. The

The locket above was a gift to Abigail from John Adams as he left for France in 1778. The fatalistic inscription reads, "I yield whatever is is right."

party spread to the other ships when they arrived. This time John Adams approved.

The ministers of George III responded to the Boston Tea Party by passing the "Intolerable Acts," which closed Boston Harbor and appointed a military governor for Massachusetts. Although the sternest provisions were aimed at New England, the implications of the acts were clear throughout the colonies, and in Philadelphia on September 5, 1774, the First Continental Congress convened in protest. John Adams, delegate from Massachusetts, labored for passage of the Suffolk Resolves (named for Boston's county), which advocated outright resistance to the Intolerable Acts. The Resolves were accepted, and Adams returned home one of the most influential men in the province.

At the Second Continental Congress, in 1775, John Adams was the most vigorous delegate. He urged that regionalism be sacrificed for the good of all the colonies, that each state contribute to a single continental army, that George Washington be commander of that army. He served on the committee that drew up the Declaration of Independence and was its foremost defender when it was attacked by moderates. He favored a union of states into a single government and actively backed the Articles of Confederation, which created a United States of America and remained in force until the Constitution was ratified in 1788. Adams debated almost every issue and was a member

The paintings above of Abigail Adams Smith, left, and her parents, John and Abigail Adams, were done in London in the 1780's. Ralph Earl painted Mrs. Adams; Mather Brown, the others.

of more than ninety different committees.

Past forty and rotund, Adams was not cut out for soldiering, so while the Revolution was being fought, he became a diplomat. In 1778 and again two years later he was sent to France, but he got along with neither Benjamin Franklin, the American minister, nor the Comte de Vergennes, the French foreign minister. In The Hague, however, Adams successfully negotiated a large loan in 1782. Then he returned to France, where with Franklin and Jay on September 3, 1783, he signed the Treaty of Paris, wherein Great Britain acknowledged the existence of a separate and independent United States of America. Two years later he became the first American minister to the Court of St. James's. In London, John Adams was a proud, aggressive, uncompromising defender of American interests. But his approach to the British probably made little difference, for almost every American attempt to establish friendship and commercial relations with England was received coldly. In 1788, after three frustrating years in London, Adams asked to be recalled.

When he arrived home a new government was being formed under the recently ratified Constitution. Adams believed—and he was by no means alone in his belief—that the Vice Presidency belonged to him almost as automatically as the Presidency did to George Washington; but while the General was elected unanimously, Adams won with a plurality of only 34 out of 69 electoral votes. The widely distributed balloting was engineered by Alexander Hamilton, who thereby planted the seeds of a feud from which neither man would profit.

Adams' attempts to interpret and define the responsibilities of the Vice Presidency as presented in the Constitution were complicated by his concern with petty details. He pondered whether he should be his own man or the President's, whether he should be an independent statesman in the Senate, over which he presided, or an impartial monitor. He asked the Senate for advice: should he address the chamber standing or sitting? "Gentlemen," he said, "I am possessed of two separate powers—the one in *esse*, the other in *passe* [Vice President of the United States but President of the Senate] . . . when the President comes into the Senate, what shall I be?" Who cares? thought Senator William Maclay, a huge, rugged Pennsylvania lawyer, advocate of democratic simplicity and keeper of the journal that gives us our most thorough glimpse into the early years of the Senate. Adams was fond of official titles, without which, he thought, "governments cannot be raised nor supported." Writing that Adams "may go and dream about titles, for he will get none," Maclay and his side prevailed. But behind his back, some senators did acquiesce in the

Vice President's affection for titles by awarding him one of his own: His Rotundity.

With the matter of titles settled against him, Adams, according to Maclay, continued to infuriate the Senate with his condescension. Before debate on any issue could begin, the Vice President insisted on addressing to the chamber a lecture on the constitutional responsibilities of the Senate. During debate, he was arbitrary and prejudiced in his decisions regarding who could and who could not participate. Before a vote could be taken, he would, like a schoolmaster talking to children, summarize the issue, or his own interpretation of it, and unhesitatingly instruct the senators how to vote.

By philosophy Adams was a Federalist. He did not trust the masses, and he acknowledged a "natural division [between] the gentlemen and the simple men." But by temperament he was simply not a party man. However opinionated he might have been, he was not faithful to ideological dogma. Hamilton seems to have gathered as much, and throughout Washington's first administration, he looked for signs of the Vice President's unreliability. As Senate president, Adams had broken twenty tie votes—all in accordance with the position of Washington, who more often than not sided with the Hamiltonians. Therefore, Hamilton had no grounds on which to oppose Adams.

Adams stood for re-election because he wanted to be President. In his second term in the second office, he had less to do—there were fewer tie votes—and he came to hate the job. Once he had been a mover of events, a great debater, a figure in controversy; now he was a loyal, passive observer. To Abigail he wrote, "My country has in its wisdom contrived for me the most insignificant office that ever the invention of man contrived or his imagination conceived."

The election of 1796 was the first bipartisan election in the United States. The Constitution had made no provisions for parties, and candidates were selected by congressional caucus. Candidates for the Presidency and Vice Presidency were listed together on a ballot that did not differentiate between the offices. Each elector voted twice, and the highest and next-highest vote getters became President and Vice President. The Federalists nominated Adams and Thomas Pinckney; the Democratic-Republicans, Jefferson and Aaron Burr. Wanting to be the power behind the President and anticipating that he would never be able to control Adams, Hamilton quietly worked for the election of Pinckney to the Presidency. His own power, however, was less than he had estimated, and his plan backfired. Adams won, but by just three votes, and Jefferson became Vice President.

The circumstances under which Adams took office could hardly have been worse. In the first place, he succeeded the Father of His Country—a tough act to follow. To Adams it was unjust that he should have to wallow in the muck of party politics that George Washington had for the most part been able to remain above. But wallow he did: unlike Washington—the living legend, the gallant warrior—Adams, the chubby intellectual, could find no support in the idolizing masses. Forced to seek support from the party, he retained Washington's largely Hamiltonian Cabinet—a mistake. Finally, Adams was saddled with a Vice President who had not wanted the office and who belonged to—indeed led—the opposition.

By taking Jefferson into his confidence, Adams hoped that they could labor together effectively. But a gap had developed between them. Jefferson had read articles by Adams condemning some aspects of the French Revolution and had called Adams a monarchist. His son John Quincy Adams had written answers to the Jefferson-endorsed works of Thomas Paine; when reissued, the articles were attributed to the elder Adams, and the gap was broadened. At the outset of their administration, as the crisis with France intensified, their mutual desire to avoid war might have succeeded in closing the rift to some extent; but after Jefferson, on the grounds that the Vice President belonged to the legislative branch of the government and could not participate in executive discussions, refused to go to

France as a special envoy, they seldom saw each other. They were further estranged on the issue of the Naturalization, Alien, and Sedition Acts, and by the end of the administration, the President and Jefferson were not even on speaking terms.

Adams also tried to get on with Alexander Hamilton, but that did not work either. Hamilton simply could not rid himself of the notion that every presidential concession meant that Adams might be handled. A cycle developed: the President would give an inch, Hamilton would take a foot, and Adams the next time would give nothing at all. Adams' persistence and courage could take the form of either stubborn inflexibility or admirable determination—depending on whom he was dealing with—but on the surface he retained that old air of shyness that Hamilton could not see through. The Adams-Hamilton conflict marred the whole of the administration and wrecked the political future of Adams, Hamilton, and the Federalist party.

The crisis with France was the principal issue of Adams' administration. For his part, Adams was not sympathetic to the French revolutionists, but he had long been biased against Great Britain; so he immediately became a man in the middle. By nature, the Federalists favored aristocratic England; and the Democratic-Republicans, revolutionary France. France itself regarded the United States as favorable to Britain, especially since the completion of Jay's Treaty, and the Federalist-dominated Congress did little to contradict the French impression. In France, citizens with pro-American sympathies were imprisoned; the French assumed that every American vessel was bound toward a British port; and when Adams dispatched General Charles Pinckney to Paris to see what could be done about stopping French harassment of American ships, Talleyrand, the French foreign minister, refused to see him. The Hamiltonians were poised for battle, and the President urged an increase in the strength of the armed forces. Determined to negotiate before firing, however, Adams tried diplomacy again, dispatching Pinckney and two other ministers to Paris. Talleyrand sent a trio of his own to see them under a cloak of carefully contrived secrecy. In confidential undertones, the French agents said that Talleyrand would listen favorably to any American proposal if the United States would issue a large loan to France and make Talleyrand's attentions worth his while. Informed of the attempted blackmail, Adams sent the diplomats' report to Congress, but for the names of the French agents, he substituted the initials X, Y, and Z. Congress released the report to the public, which became infected with what Jefferson called the XYZ fever, a national passion to avenge the French insult. Always anti-French, Hamilton fed the militant attitude, writing that any defender of France was "a fool, a madman, or a traitor."

He implied, of course, that John Adams was one or all of these. Although the President was in favor of preparedness—he signed military appropriations and urged George Washington to resume command of the armed services—he was not himself stricken with XYZ fever. Still determined to negotiate, he insisted on Talleyrand's assurance that representatives of the United States would be treated with courtesy in Paris. Thoroughly embarrassed by the furor that the XYZ Affair had caused, the French minister agreed, reasoning that further hostility toward the United States would simply provide England with another ally. Another American minister to the French Republic was dispatched (over the objections of Hamilton, who later pressured Adams into changing the delegation to a mission of three, two of whom were Hamiltonians); and with the Treaty of Morfontaine on September 30, 1800, the good relations between the United States and France were restored. The settlement had great personal value for Adams, who soon after its conclusion composed his own epitaph: "Here lies John Adams, who took upon himself the responsibility of the peace with France in the year 1800."

The Federalist party was badly shaken by the XYZ Affair. Hamilton had expected that congressional passage of military bills would inspire France to declare war, thereby

In the print above, L'Insurgente *surrenders to the* U.S.S. Constellation *in 1799. America captured eighty-four French vessels in the undeclared war.*

discrediting the pro-French Republicans. That, of course, had not worked. Moreover, the Republican press had called the whole affair a hoax, insinuating that the diplomats whose report had fostered the XYZ fever had made themselves unavailable to conciliation. Adams received blows from both sides —from the Federalists for not going to war with France and from the Republicans for stimulating panic by promoting congressional passage of the military bills.

In 1798, the majority Federalists tried to utilize the national enthusiasm for war to silence their critics; they sponsored and passed the Naturalization, Alien, and Sedition Acts. During the height of the French crisis, Frenchmen in America were widely assumed to favor their homeland, while many non-French Europeans were known to sympathize with the principles of the French Revolution. Forgetting—or choosing to ignore—the similarity between the French and the American struggles for independence, the Federalists first passed the Naturalization Act, raising the period of residency required for American citizenship to fourteen years. Then came the Alien Act, which gave the President power to expel all foreigners he considered dangerous, and the Alien Enemies Act, which gave him the right to deport or imprison any native of a nation at war with the United States. Finally, the Sedition Act forbade "insurrection, riot, unlawful assembly" and prescribed fines and jail terms for "false, scandalous and malicious writing" about the President, Congress, or nation. A case can be made for the necessity of such legislation, but the Federalists employed the acts to silence opponents. Closing their ranks against what they considered an assault on freedom of speech and the press, the Jeffersonians declared that the Alien and Sedition Acts were violations of constitutionally guaranteed rights. State courts were urged to disregard the acts, and many did.

The Alien and Sedition Acts conformed with the political philosophy of John Adams, and he signed them, thus losing what little Republican admiration his stand on France had won him; but the instinctive, sensitive Adams in practice ignored them, thereby giving Hamilton fresh ammunition. In fact, Hamilton himself had grave doubts about the constitutionality of the Alien and Sedition Acts, but he could not resist the opportunity to abuse the President. When Adams failed to deport Joseph Priestly, an English radical whose outspoken advocacy of the French Revolution had scandalized the Federalists, and when he pardoned John Fries, who had been condemned to death for leading a violent Pennsylvania uprising against the war taxes voted in 1798, Hamilton wrote an open *Letter Concerning the Public Conduct and Character of John Adams*. Dealing mostly with the President's handling of the French crisis, the document was too obscure to be read by the simple people and too illogical to impress the nation's leaders. It did, however, have disastrous results for Adams.

His administration had been stormy, but Adams was cautiously optimistic about winning the second term he so desperately wanted. He had purged his Cabinet of two Hamiltonian spies, his generosity regarding the Alien and Sedition Acts defendants had by and large compensated for his earlier unpopular support of the acts, and the peace with France had deprived the Jeffersonians of a monumental issue. But when Hamilton's letter was published, Adams' optimism was dissipated, for if the document was an almost meaningless hodgepodge of unreadable rhetoric, it was also a crystal-clear statement that the Federalists were deeply divided. The letter irritated even Charles Pinckney, the Hamiltonian "vice presidential" candidate in 1800, who, to his credit, announced that he would not be a party to a plan to divert votes from Adams.

Meanwhile, the White House, though far from finished, was ready for occupancy. Abigail was ill, and Adams arrived from Philadelphia without her. On November 1, 1800, he became the first Chief Executive to sleep in the Mansion. Reflecting on the potential of the White House as a symbol in the affections of Americans, he composed a prayer that Franklin Delano Roosevelt later had carved on the mantel of the State Dining Room: "I pray Heaven to bestow the best of Blessings on this House and all that shall hereafter inhabit it. May none but honest and wise men ever rule under this roof." When Mrs. Adams finally arrived, she hung a clothesline and a Stuart portrait of George Washington; the outcome of the election would determine what else she would do.

Adams and Pinckney were opposed again by Jefferson and Burr, and Burr's powerful New York machine proved decisive. The President had no trouble at all placing the blame for his defeat: "Mr. Hamilton has carried his eggs to a fine market," he wrote. "The very two men of all the world that he was most jealous of are now placed over him." In a letter to a friend Adams confided that his defeat was a good thing, as he expected to die soon. His last official act was the appointment of John Marshall as Chief Justice of the Supreme Court.

Disappointed and bitter, Adams left Washington by stagecoach on the morning of Jefferson's inauguration, conspicuously absenting himself from it. Retiring to Quincy (formerly Braintree), Massachusetts, he became a farmer, insisting that he had not been so cheerful "since some sin to me unknown involved me in politics." He gathered together his diaries and started work on an autobiography.

Perhaps his affront to Jefferson bothered him, for on the first day of 1812, Adams wrote a genial letter to Monticello. "I wish you Sir many happy New Years and that you may enter the next and many succeeding Years with as animating Prospects for the Public as those at present before Us." He signed it "Friend," and Jefferson—by what was almost return mail in those days—wrote back on January 21: "A letter from you calls up recollections very dear to my mind. It carries me back to the times when, beset with difficulties and dangers, we were fellow laborers in the same cause, struggling for what is most valuable to man, his right of self-government." The two ex-Presidents thus began an extensive correspondence, exchanging ideas about current affairs from time to time, but devoting themselves mainly to nostalgic reminiscences or philosophical bantering. Jefferson shared Adams' misery when Abigail died of typhoid in 1818, and Adams' joy when John Quincy Adams was elected President of the United States.

John Adams died at ninety on, appropriately, the Fourth of July, 1826, the fiftieth anniversary of the Declaration of Independence. His last words were "Jefferson still survives." But Jefferson in fact did not. He had died at Monticello several hours earlier.

—DAVID JACOBS

John Adams

A PICTURE PORTFOLIO

John Adams' spectacles lie on the tulipwood desk bought when he was in Europe. The desk is now at the family home in Quincy, Massachusetts.

THE BOSTON MASSACRE

John Adams was thirty-five when he undertook as important a case as any ever "tried in any court or country of the world." With typical dramatic flair the young attorney thus described his upcoming defense of the officer and soldiers indicted for murder in the Boston Massacre of 1770. Adams for some time had foreseen the inevitable clash of military and citizenry: with the British troop buildups that followed the colonists' protests against English tax measures, Adams had said that the danger "appeared in full view before me." He viewed his acceptance of the case as a kind of martyrdom, for the defendants' cause was universally unpopular. But shortly before the trial began he was chosen a Boston delegate to the General Court, the electorate apparently acknowledging his courage and integrity in the delicate legal situation. The jury acquitted six soldiers, and the remaining two received token punishment. Adams could rest assured that justice and the law had been served. But the radical press of John's cousin Sam Adams, disappointed at the loss of a guilty verdict and a propaganda plum, upbraided Adams in the months that followed. After one term in the General Court, Adams retired to Braintree, declaring himself "an infirm man" and feeling much put upon. Yet he could not long remain detached from public life, and by 1774 he was named a Massachusetts delegate to the Continental Congress in Philadelphia, where he would help to shape a new nation.

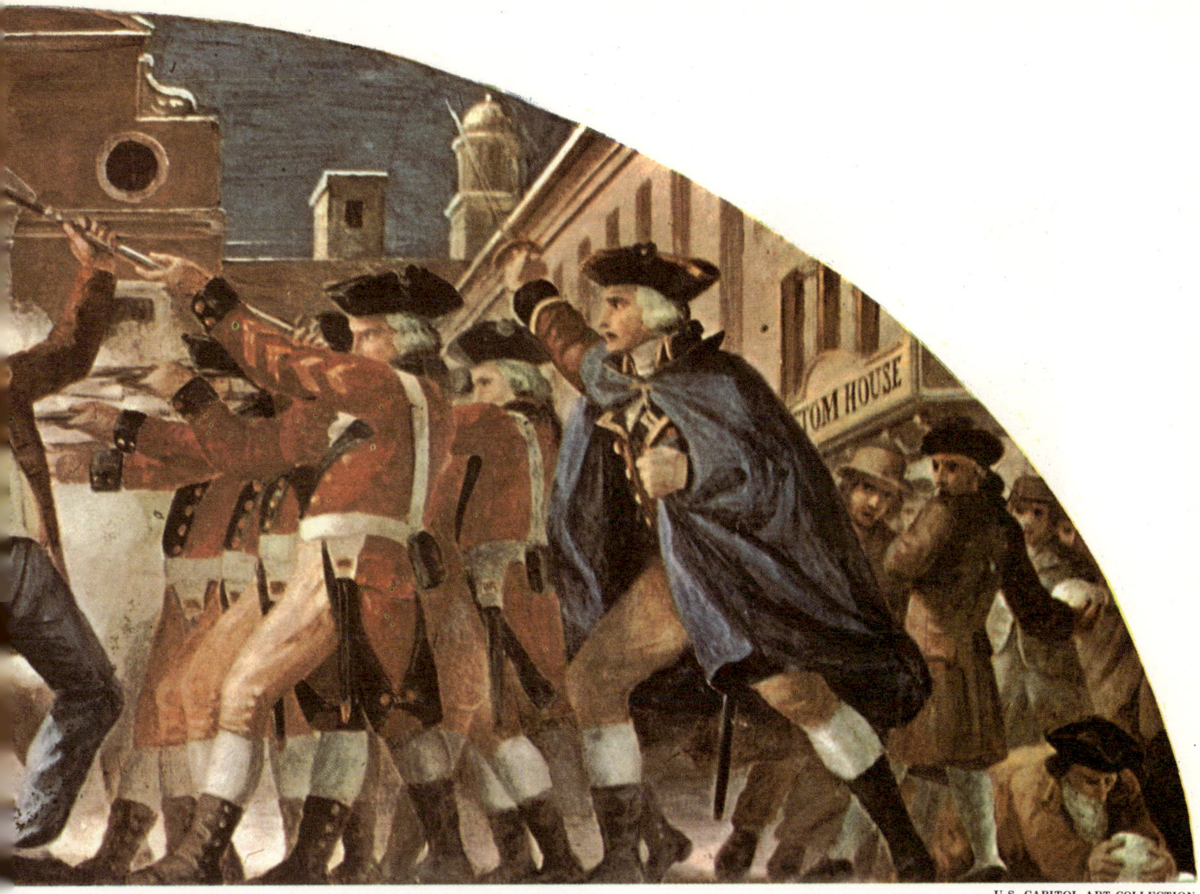

U.S. CAPITOL ART COLLECTION

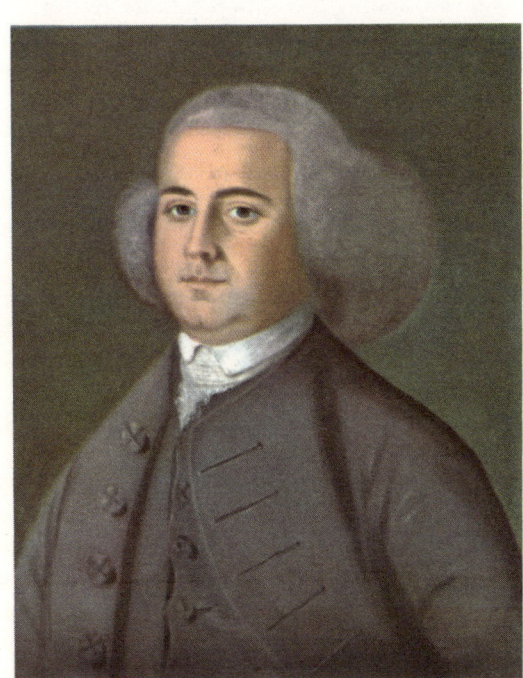

MASSACHUSETTS HISTORICAL SOCIETY

The fresco above of the Boston Massacre is located in the National Capitol. It depicts the height of the crisis: one of the mob has been shot, and the redcoats, taunted by the angry crowd, continue their retaliation.

The portrait at left by Benjamin Blyth shows John Adams in 1776. At thirty-one, he was a prominent attorney.

The stamp below was authorized under the hated Stamp Act of 1765, the first direct taxation of the colonies by the Crown. Stamps were required for all newspapers, pamphlets, and legal documents. Violent protests ensued, and the seeds of permanent dissension were sown.

NEW YORK PUBLIC LIBRARY

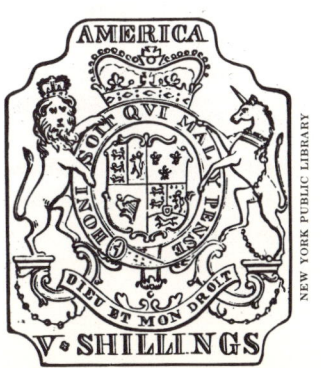

MASSACHUSETTS PATRIOTS

JOHN HANCOCK

John Hancock, one of the most influential financiers of the patriot cause, became a popular hero in 1768 when he was charged with smuggling wine into Boston in violation of an English tax measure. With John Adams pleading the defense, the case dragged on for months until it was finally withdrawn by the Crown's attorneys. The following year Hancock, then twenty-two, was elected to the first of several terms in the General Court. In 1773 he took part in exposing letters, written by Governor Thomas Hutchinson, that vilified the colonies. The court became the Provincial Congress in 1774, and Hancock twice was its president. He married Dorothy Quincy in 1775 and went on to serve two terms as president of the Continental Congress and to sign the Declaration of Independence; because of the prominence of his name on that document, "John Hancock" has become a synonym for "signature." Hancock had military aspirations, but his only participation in the war was to command a force from Massachusetts in a Rhode Island campaign of 1788. Boston's leading merchant, he was elected in 1780 to the first of nine terms as governor of the new state. He was president of the convention to ratify the federal Constitution in 1788. He died at fifty-six in 1793.

SAMUEL ADAMS

His cousin Sam, John Adams said, was a "universal good character . . . [but was] too attentive to the public, and not enough to himself and his family." Born in Boston in 1722, Sam Adams was recklessly overgenerous as far back as anyone could remember: the first time he had enough money to go into business, he promptly "loaned" half of it to an eminently undependable friend. As the cause of American independence began to occupy him, he gave less thought than ever to his own affairs. He secured a job as tax collector and refused to collect the taxes he thought unjust. While his bills mounted and his house and clothing grew shabbier, he helped organize the Sons of Liberty, became a radical leader in the Massachusetts legislature, and inspired the Boston Tea Party. While his friends bought him clothing and repaired his house, Sam went off to attend the First and Second Continental Congresses. After independence had been won, he served in Congress and later as governor of Massachusetts. Perhaps the most significant thing about Samuel Adams was his effect on other men. He could arouse the passions of the farmer and the laborer, but he could also drive the stuffiness from intellectuals like John Adams, whose commitment to the Revolution was prodded into the open by his cousin.

PAUL REVERE

Paul Revere spent his early years as a silversmith, a trade he had learned in his father's shop, but in 1765 the thirty-year-old artisan began a series of political cartoons that were effective patriot propaganda and brought him into association with Samuel Adams, John Hancock, and other Revolutionary leaders. Revere was sent to New York and Philadelphia in 1774 to seek support for Boston's protests against the Intolerable Acts, which England had passed in retaliation for the Boston Tea Party. Late that year he led a raid on British munitions at Fort William and Mary. On April 16, 1775, Revere rode to Concord to warn of an impending raid on the colonial arsenal there; two nights later he sped to Lexington to tell Sam Adams and Hancock that they were marked men and to alert the citizenry that British troops were on the move. In 1776, he became a member of the Committee of Correspondence, which coordinated the colonies' resistance efforts. Revere saw little fighting during the war, but was commissioned to design the first Continental currency, and for a time he manufactured gunpowder. Returning to peacetime pursuits in 1782, Revere resumed making the excellent silver pieces for which he is properly renowned. He died in Boston in 1818.

JAMES OTIS

This portrait of James Otis gives no hint of the volatility and white-hot passion which were at once an inspiration to American patriots and a harbinger of the insanity of his later years. In 1743 Otis, eighteen, graduated from Harvard; he studied law with Jeremiah Gridley and began practice in Boston in 1750. He served briefly as the Crown's attorney general and then as advocate general of the vice-admiralty court. After resigning the latter post, he argued the case against the hated Writs of Assistance in 1761. Otis lost, but he stood his ground. In 1763 he made a speech in which he said that a higher law superseded Parliament's, that Americans were, "by the laws of God and Nature, entitled to all the essential Privileges of Britons." His views were to serve as guidelines for American political theory. One of the prime political leaders of Massachusetts during the 1760's, he served on the General Court, attended the Stamp Act Congress, and affiliated himself with the Sons of Liberty. Though he always urged only "dutiful and loyal Addresses" to the Crown, Otis' urgency and orotund power made men, as John Adams noted, "ready to take up arms." His zeal giving way to incipient insanity, Otis retired in 1771. He was killed by a bolt of lightning in 1783.

The painting below, probably by John Trumbull, is the quintessence of Ben Franklin, diplomat. Parisian high society had never encountered anyone quite like him: he blended the elements of simple American frontiersman (complete with coonskin hat) with charming and sophisticated conversation and an unerring sense of timing. He captivated statesman and citizen alike, and he was undeniably a great favorite with the ladies of court society. John Adams said that he could "never obtain the favor of [his] company in a morning before breakfast."

YALE UNIVERSITY ART GALLERY

"A FRIEND TO HUMAN KIND"

He was seventy years old, and though he had "retired" almost three decades before, Benjamin Franklin found himself clomping down the ship's ramp onto French soil on behalf of his country. He had come to ask for help—for support and money—and all his talk about what France might gain from American independence would be just so much salesmanship; nevertheless, the French were delighted to see him. They displayed his portrait in shop windows, stamped his image on coins and jewelry, held banquets in his honor. When John Adams arrived two years later, in 1778, he was astonished. Franklin's reputation, he noted, was so universal that "there was scarcely a peasant or a citizen, a *valet de chambre*, coachman or footman, a lady's chambermaid or a scullion in a kitchen who was not familiar with it, and who did not consider him a friend to human kind."

Europe had known Ben Franklin for a long time. *Poor Richard's Almanack* had been translated, his scientific experiments widely duplicated, and even the great Mozart had composed an adagio for the armonica, a musical instrument of Franklin's invention. But France held a special admiration for the Philadelphian, for while Franklin suited their romantic portrait of the wise and simple American, he also belonged alongside Voltaire and Defoe and Montesquieu in the Age of Enlightenment, that international phenomenon which France thought purely French.

Franklin was wise but by no account simple, and he was perfectly willing to accept the role in which the French had cast him. Before long, John Adams grew impatient with Franklin; Adams had come to deal in diplomacy, not to participate in "continual dissipation," nor to dress like a Daniel Boone and recite little wisdoms. Openly critical, he deplored the Franklin-led commission, its waste and inefficiency, and he was recalled. What John Adams had neglected to consider was that Benjamin Franklin was accomplishing a great deal.

Adams could not even enjoy the luxury of being alone with his resentment during the voyage home; instead, he was accompanied by a French official gushing admiration for Franklin. At one point Adams erupted: "It is universally believed in France, England and all of Europe," he said, "that his electric wand has accomplished this Revolution. But nothing is more groundless. He has done very little."

Adams returned to Europe in 1780 and negotiated a Dutch loan large enough to reduce American dependency on France. This proved valuable during the Paris peace negotiations, for Franklin had in fact become overly acquiescent to French plans to participate in the talks. France would be better served by a continuing war between the United States and Great Britain than by American independence; thus Adams and the third American commissioner, John Jay, overruled Franklin's efforts to have the French present at the parleys. The treaty was concluded in 1783 with a minimum of French interference.

Franklin irritated Adams even after his death in 1790. While the aura around Franklin's name grew, John Adams insisted that he had been "the vainest man and the falsest character I have ever met with. . . ."

The Adams house, opposite, is shown as it appeared in 1787, when John bought it for some £600. Dr. Cotton Tufts, Abigail's uncle, negotiated the transaction while Adams was minister to the Court of St. James's. The house was constructed in 1731.

The china used by the Adams family in the White House in 1800 (left) is now displayed at Peacefield.

Adams' first addition to the house was an extension containing the Long Room (below). The furniture, purchased in France, was the first to be used in the White House. The portraits of Abigail, John Quincy, and John are copies of originals now hanging in the Executive Mansion in Washington.

ALL: ADAMS NATIONAL HISTORIC SITE

PEACEFIELD

In 1787, John Adams was anxious to get home. He had been ambassador to England for two years and a diplomat in Europe for seven before that. His latest post had brought only disappointment; a lasting amity with Britain seemed as far away as ever, and in 1788 he resigned. Although he and Abigail were eager to return to Massachusetts, they must have been somewhat uneasy about the house they were to occupy, for they had bought it unseen while still in England. The modest home was in Braintree, and contained only a paneled parlor and dining room on the ground floor and two bedrooms and three smaller rooms above. The kitchen and servants' quarters were in a separate building. Abigail said at first sight that the building looked like "a wren's house."

The Adamses were not to remain long at Peacefield, as John named it, for with the election of 1789 and John's ascension to the Vice Presidency they soon would be living in New York. The seat of government shortly would shift to Philadelphia, and through the 1790's John Adams spent little time at Peacefield except for periodic visits. During his Presidency, Adams added to the house a gabled extension, including the Long Room on the ground floor and a capacious second-story study. Since farming was a lifelong delight to Adams, he also erected a complex of barns and stables.

John Adams retired happily to Quincy following his Presidency; he had twenty-six years to devote to family, farming, and correspondence. Subsequent Adams generations made their own contributions to the Old House, as it came to be called, notably a stone library, adjacent to the house, for John Quincy's books and letters, and the connection of the kitchen to the main building. The house was last used as a residence in 1927 and now is a national historic site.

The love that filled the early-nineteenth-century jug at left was a bipartisan liquid, intended for the lips of both Federalist Thees and Republican Thines. To one side of the message is a portrait of John Adams, and to the other, a picture of James Madison.

In his magnanimous letter (below) to John Adams after the presidential election of 1796, Thomas Jefferson lashed out at mutual adversary Alexander Hamilton, who had tried to subvert Adams' victory. At the advice of Democratic-Republican party organizer James Madison, however, the letter was never sent.

Dear Sir   Monticello Dec. 28. 1796

The public & the public papers have been much occupied lately in placing us in a point of opposition to each other. I trust with confidence that less of it has been felt by ourselves personally. in the retired canton where I am, I learn little of what is passing: pamphlets I see never; papers but a few; and the fewer the happier. our latest intelligence from Philadelphia at present is of the 16th inst. but tho' at that date your election to the first magistracy seems not to have been known as a fact, yet with me it has never been doubted. I knew it impossible you should lose a vote North of the Delaware, & even if that of Pennsylvania should be against you in the mass, yet that you would get enough South of that to place your succession out of danger. I have never one single moment expected a different issue; & tho' I know I shall not be believed, yet it is not the less true that I have never wished it. my neighbors, as my compurgators, could aver that fact, because they see my occupations & my attachment to them. indeed it is possible that you may be cheated of your succession by the trick worthy the subtlety of your arch-friend of New York, who has been able to make of your real friends tools to defeat their & your just wishes. most probably he will be disappointed as to you, & my inclinations place me out of his reach. I leave to

THOMAS PINCKNEY

FRIENDLY RIVALS

Y ou and I," wrote Vice President John Adams to Thomas Jefferson in 1796, "must look down from the battlements of heaven if we ever have the pleasure of seeing it." From Monticello, Jefferson answered that he agreed, adding that politics was "a subject I never loved and now hate." The two men were both nominees in the first contested presidential election of the young nation's life, and they saw no reason to alter their cordial twenty-year-long relationship. Meanwhile, a Democratic-Republican handbill in wide circulation asserted that *"Thomas Jefferson . . .* first framed the sacred political sentence that all men are *born* equal. *John Adams* says this is all farce and falsehood. . . . Which of these . . . will you have for your President?" The Federalist press, in turn, called Jefferson an enemy of the Constitution, an atheist, freethinker, and coward. Just as President Washington had feared, "the daemon of party spirit" penetrated American politics and possessed the election. But while their countrymen spat venom at one another, the two principal candidates, aloof from the indignity of campaigning, continued when they could their old correspondence. The election results were predictably regional: Jefferson's strength came from the South, Adams' from the North, and they shared the Middle Atlantic states. Adams won, but Jefferson, with just three electoral votes fewer, became Vice President.

Because John Adams' relationship with the Federalist party was more an alliance than allegiance, Alexander Hamilton tried to arrange the election so that the vice presidential candidate, Thomas Pinckney, would be elected President. Hamilton, however, was not always a perceptive judge of men, and Pinckney later proved less faithful to the party than Adams: he was an advocate of states' rights; he not only opposed Hamilton's efforts to have war declared with France, but he was against Adams' military build-up during the crisis; and as a congressman from South Carolina, he voted against the Sedition Act. Born in Charleston in 1750, Pinckney was raised and educated in England, graduating from Oxford. He returned to South Carolina and became an officer in the militia in 1775. After the Revolution, he was appointed minister to Great Britain, where he served until 1795, when he was sent to Spain to negotiate a settlement of U.S.-Spanish borders in North America. Returning home a year later, he probably would have won the Vice Presidency but for Hamilton's meddling. When the New England electors heard that Hamilton was trying to secure more votes for Pinckney than for Adams, they cast their votes for Adams and Jefferson, and Pinckney received only fifty-nine votes. After two terms in Congress (1797–1801), he quit politics and devoted his life to agriculture until his death in 1828.

YEARS OF TURMOIL

After the Alien and Sedition Acts were passed in 1798, a Newark man was fined one hundred dollars for wishing out loud that a cannon wadding would lodge in the President's backside; a county official in New York was manacled and driven two hundred miles to jail for his anti-administration remarks; Congressman Matthew Lyon of Vermont was sentenced to four months for calling Adams pompous and selfish in a personal letter. But the Federalist "Reign of Terror" was short lived: so harsh was the wording of the acts that just being a Republican was almost tantamount to sedition, and there were too many Republicans to jail them all. Public outrage began working against the Federalists. Representative Lyon was easily re-elected while serving his jail term. Vice President Jefferson made capital of the widespread indignation, spread a rumor that the Federalists were about to crown Adams king, and convinced the Kentucky and Virginia legislatures to declare the acts unconstitutional and therefore inapplicable in those states. The uproar dimmed national interest in the undeclared naval war with France and overshadowed Adams' successful peace negotiations. Condemned by the Republicans for signing the Alien and Sedition Acts and disowned by most Federalists for making peace with France, Adams was through. A Federalist congressman said he hoped the President would break his neck; he was not charged with sedition. The elections came and Adams went, the Alien and Sedition Acts went, and so did Federalist possession of the Presidency forever.

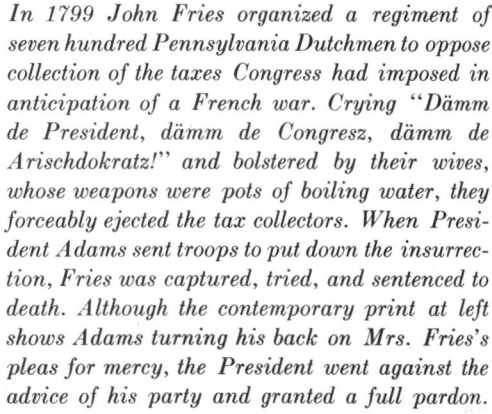

In 1799 John Fries organized a regiment of seven hundred Pennsylvania Dutchmen to oppose collection of the taxes Congress had imposed in anticipation of a French war. Crying "Dämm de President, dämm de Congresz, dämm de Arischdokratz!" and bolstered by their wives, whose weapons were pots of boiling water, they forceably ejected the tax collectors. When President Adams sent troops to put down the insurrection, Fries was captured, tried, and sentenced to death. Although the contemporary print at left shows Adams turning his back on Mrs. Fries's pleas for mercy, the President went against the advice of his party and granted a full pardon.

Although Congress never declared war against France, it could not resist the temptation to commemorate a victorious battle. In 1800, the congressional medal shown above was awarded to Thomas Truxton, commander of the Constellation. It shows his frigate pursuing France's *La Vengeance*, which was subsequently captured.

In 1798, Federalist Roger Griswold insulted Republican Matthew Lyon in the House of Representatives, and Lyon spat in his face. Two weeks later, Griswold struck back with his cane; Lyon picked up the fireplace tongs, and Congress' first good brawl (left) was under way.

83

John Adams' most ambitious, exhausting, and often frustrating efforts during his Presidency were devoted to making peace with France. When the Treaty of Morfontaine was signed in 1800, he regarded it as the single achievement for which he should most be remembered.

Artists Francesco and J. B. Piranesi, uncle and nephew, may well have been witnesses to the signing of the treaty, for their studio was in Morfontaine. Their hand-colored print, above, illustrates the festivities of October 3, 1800, in honor of the conclusion of the crisis.

FEDERAL CITY

In 1790 Congress authorized the establishment of a permanent seat for the national government. The act provided for the transfer of operations from Philadelphia to Washington (which the President always called "Federal City") in 1800, but no one could foresee the frustrations and delays which would attend the ambitious project. The builders' efforts were continually thwarted by supply and labor shortages and by congressional frugality. The lawmakers and the Supreme Court were wedged into the lone completed wing of the Capitol; the congressmen were "utterly secluded from Society" in the sparsely populated city. At the other end of muddy Pennsylvania Avenue, Abigail Adams found the unfinished White House damp, chilly, and ill-lit. But as the century progressed, the Potomac tract blossomed, as Washington had once envisioned, into a model of "Grandeur, Simplicity and Convenience."

Irish-born James Hoban won $500 for his design for the Executive Mansion (above). His competitors included Thomas Jefferson and Capitol designer William Thornton, whose plans also reflected the mid-eighteenth-century Palladian style. Construction on Washington's oldest public building began in 1792, but it was not completed by the 1800 deadline.

This serene vista (left), from an 1801 engraving, depicts a Georgetown-Federal City area quite different from that described by John and Abigail Adams when, in November of 1800, they became the first First Family to occupy the President's permanent residence. Abigail found Georgetown the "very dirtiest hole I ever saw," and was candid in her reactions to the stump-strewn landscape and the swampy nature of field and road alike. She allowed, perhaps ambiguously, that the region was indeed "capable of every improvement."

As construction lagged, the Capitol could boast only a north wing, as seen in the 1800 water color below by William Birch.

LIBRARY OF CONGRESS

LIBRARY OF CONGRESS

FACTS IN SUMMARY: JOHN ADAMS

CHRONOLOGY

UNITED STATES		ADAMS			
	1735	Born October 19		1783	Signs Treaty of Paris
	1751	Enters Harvard		1784	Named minister to England
French and Indian War	1754		Constitutional Convention	1787	
	1758	Admitted to the bar	Constitution ratified	1788	Returns to U.S.
James Otis opposes Writs of Assistance	1761		Washington elected President	1789	Elected Vice President
Sugar Act	1764	Marries Abigail Smith	Bill of Rights		
Stamp Act	1765	Denounces Stamp Act	Emergence of rival parties	1791	
Townshend Acts	1767				
Boston Massacre	1770	Elected to General Court		1792	Re-elected Vice President
		Defends Thomas Preston	Neutrality Proclamation	1793	
Boston Tea Party	1773		Whisky Rebellion	1794	
Intolerable Acts	1774	Delegate to First Continental Congress	Jay's Treaty		
First Continental Congress			Suspension of Franco-American relations	1796	Elected President
Lexington and Concord	1775	Delegate to Second Continental Congress		1797	Appoints commission to negotiate with French
Bunker Hill					
Second Continental Congress		Nominates Washington as commander in chief	Undeclared naval war with France	1798	XYZ Affair
					Creates Navy Department
Declaration of Independence	1776	Signs Declaration of Independence			Appoints Washington to command Army
Burgoyne surrenders at Saratoga	1777	Elected commissioner to France			Signs Alien and Sedition Acts
Articles of Confederation adopted			Fries Uprising	1799	Appoints second commission to France
			Death of Washington		
Franco-American Alliance	1778	Sails to France	Treaty of Morfontaine	1800	Moves to White House
					Loses presidential election
	1779	Returns to Boston	Jefferson inaugurated President	1801	Appoints John Marshall as Chief Justice
		Drafts Mass. constitution			
		Sails to Europe			Ends presidential term
	1780	Negotiates treaty with Netherlands	Madison elected President	1808	
Articles of Confederation ratified	1781		War with England	1812	Resumes correspondence with Jefferson
British surrender at Yorktown				1818	Death of Abigail Adams
	1782	Secures loan and recognition from Dutch	John Quincy Adams elected President	1825	
			Jefferson dies July 4	1826	Dies July 4

ADAMS NATIONAL HISTORIC SITE

A preview of VOLUME 2

In the next volume are the life stories of Thomas Jefferson, "Apostle of Americanism" and author of the Declaration of Independence; of James Madison, Chief Executive during the War of 1812; and of James Monroe, whose Presidency was called the Era of Good Feelings.

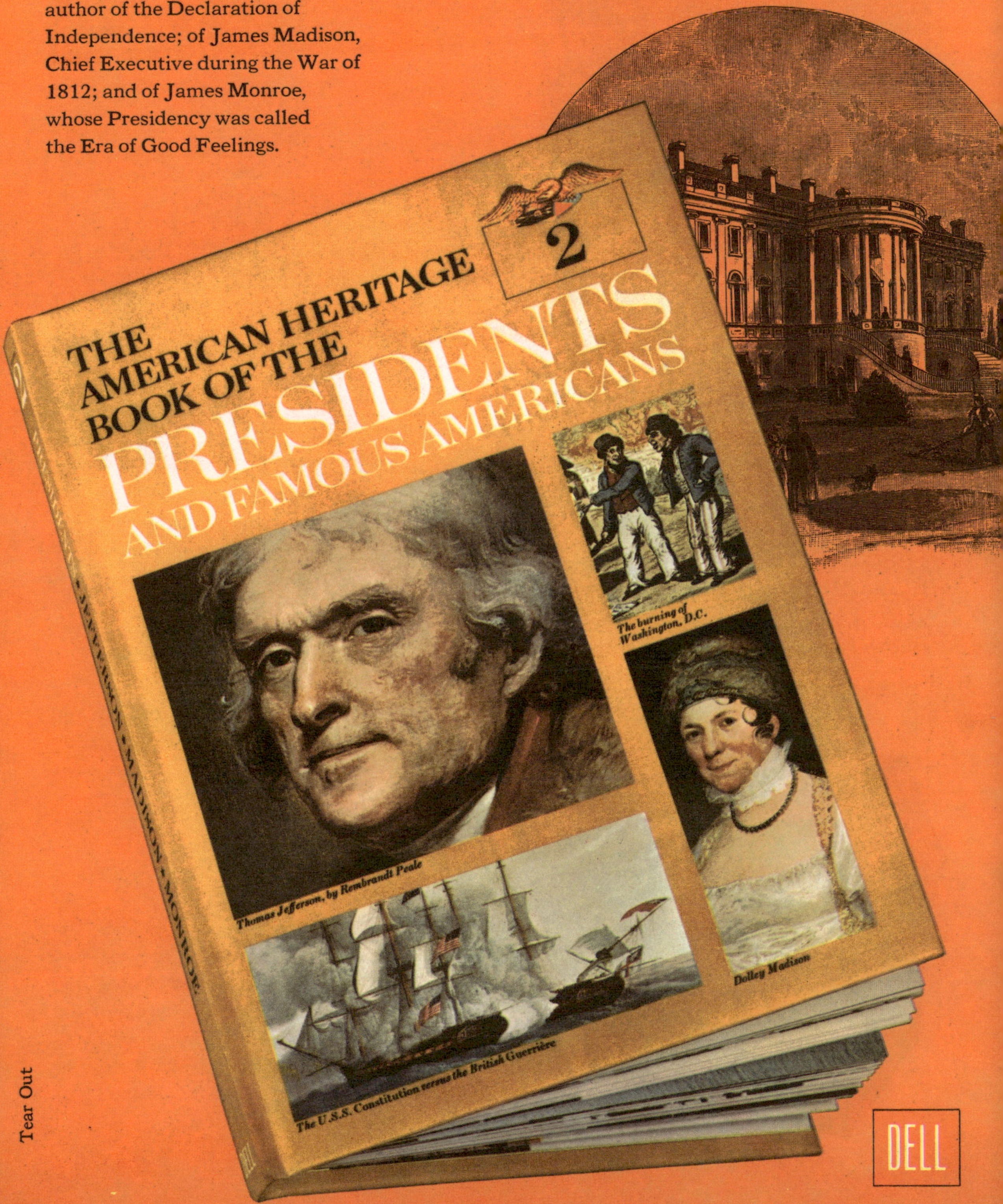

2
THE AMERICAN HERITAGE BOOK OF THE
PRESIDENTS
AND FAMOUS AMERICANS
JEFFERSON • MADISON • MONROE
The burning of Washington, D.C.
Thomas Jefferson, by Rembrandt Peale
Dolley Madison
The U.S.S. Constitution versus the British Guerrière

Tear Out

DELL

How many of these

The U.S.S. Constitution *during the War of 1812*

Above: sketches made during Lewis and Clark's danger-filled expedition to the Pacific Coast

Below: President James Monroe's liquor chest

1.

"Brittle and sickly, at five feet six and barely one hundred pounds he was the smallest of the American Presidents." Which Chief Executive does that quotation describe?

2.

Which future President crossed the Delaware River with General Washington and was wounded during the subsequent attack on the Hessians at Trenton?

3.

Which President described a group of Nobel Prize winners as "the most extraordinary collection of talent . . . that has ever been gathered together at the White House—with the possible exception of when Thomas Jefferson dined alone"?

4.

On July 4, 1826, the fiftieth anniversary of the Declaration of Independence, two former Presidents of the United States died. Who were they?

5.

"He then became involved in a scheme apparently aimed at separating at least part of the West from the United States, and conquering Mexico. Blinded by dreams of glory, he raised an army, but it was pitifully small, and he was arrested before he could do any damage." Which former Vice President is being referred to?

questions can you answer?

6.

Who said "Don't give up the ship"? When?

7.

Who was the first President ever elected by the House of Representatives?

8.

"The American continents, by the free and independent condition which they have assumed and maintain, are henceforth not to be considered as subjects for future colonization by any European power." By what name is this quotation known?

9.

Which Chief Executive described the Presidency as "a splendid misery," bringing "nothing but unceasing drudgery and daily loss of friends"?

A group of Indians danced for Monroe in 1821.

Above: two Americans watch the burning of Washington in 1814.

Below: the College of William and Mary, Jefferson's school

ANSWERS: 1. James Madison 2. James Monroe 3. John F. Kennedy 4. Thomas Jefferson and John Adams 5. Aaron Burr 6. Captain James Lawrence, before his ship, the *Chesapeake*, was sunk by the British during the War of 1812 7. Thomas Jefferson, because of a tie in the electoral vote in 1800 8. The Monroe Doctrine 9. Thomas Jefferson

FAMOUS AMERICANS

Included in Volume 2 are Meriwether Lewis and William Clark, who led the famous expedition to the Pacific; Master Commandant Oliver Perry, hero of the War of 1812; Aaron Burr, the Vice President who was later charged with treason; George Mason and Richard Henry Lee, Virginia patriots; Robert R. Livingston, who bought Louisiana for Jefferson; presidential candidate DeWitt Clinton; and the other prominent Americans shown here.

John Marshall, who was named Chief Justice by John Adams

Dolley Madison, the First Lady who had to flee from the Capital

Henry Clay, who became known as The Great Compromiser

Stephen Decatur, naval hero of wars with Tripoli and England

Patrick Henry, the Virginian who asked for liberty or death

BIOGRAPHICAL FACTS

BIRTH: Braintree (Quincy), Mass., Oct. 19, 1735
ANCESTRY: English
FATHER: John Adams; b. Braintree (Quincy), Mass., Jan. 28, 1691; d. Braintree (Quincy), Mass., May 25, 1761
FATHER'S OCCUPATION: Farmer; cordwainer
MOTHER: Susanna Boylston Adams; b. March 5, 1699; d. April 17, 1797
BROTHERS: Peter Boylston (1738–1823); Elihu (1741–1775)
WIFE: Abigail Smith; b. Weymouth, Mass., Nov. 11, 1744; d. Quincy, Mass., Oct. 28, 1818
MARRIAGE: Weymouth, Mass., Oct. 25, 1764
CHILDREN: Abigail Amelia (1765–1813); John Quincy (1767–1848); Susanna (1768–1770); Charles (1770–1800); Thomas Boylston (1772–1832)
HOME: Peacefield, Quincy, Mass.
EDUCATION: Attended private schools in Braintree; received B.A. (1755) and M.A. (1758) from Harvard
RELIGIOUS AFFILIATION: Unitarian
OCCUPATIONS BEFORE PRESIDENCY: Teacher; farmer; lawyer
PRE-PRESIDENTIAL OFFICES: Rep. to Mass. General Court; Delegate to First and Second Continental Congresses; Member of Provincial Congress of Mass.; Delegate to Mass. Constitutional Convention; Commissioner to France; Minister to Netherlands and England; Vice President
POLITICAL PARTY: Federalist
AGE AT INAUGURATION: 61
OCCUPATION AFTER PRESIDENCY: Writer
DEATH: Quincy, Mass., July 4, 1826
AGE AT DEATH: 90
PLACE OF BURIAL: First Unitarian Church, Quincy, Mass.

ELECTION OF 1796
(Each elector voted for two men.)

CANDIDATES	ELECTORAL VOTE
John Adams, Federalist	71
Thomas Jefferson, Democratic-Republican	68
Thomas Pinckney, Federalist	59
Aaron Burr, Democratic-Republican	30
Samuel Adams, Democratic-Republican	15
Oliver Ellsworth, Federalist	11
Seven others	22

Left: Adams was born in the house at right in Braintree, Massachusetts; his son John Quincy was born in the other.

UNITED STATES
March 4, 1797–March 4, 1801

United States March 4, 1797
U.S. Territory

THE ADAMS ADMINISTRATION

INAUGURATION: March 4, 1797; Federal Hall, Philadelphia
VICE PRESIDENT: Thomas Jefferson
SECRETARY OF STATE: Timothy Pickering; John Marshall (from June 6, 1800)
SECRETARY OF THE TREASURY: Oliver Wolcott, Jr.; Samuel Dexter (from Jan. 1, 1801)
SECRETARY OF WAR: James McHenry; Samuel Dexter (from June 12, 1800)
ATTORNEY GENERAL: Charles Lee
POSTMASTER GENERAL: Joseph Habersham
SECRETARY OF THE NAVY: Benjamin Stoddert
SUPREME COURT APPOINTMENTS: Bushrod Washington (1798); Alfred Moore (1799); John Marshall, Chief Justice (1801)
FIFTH CONGRESS (March 4, 1797–March 4, 1799):
Senate: 20 Federalists; 12 Democratic-Republicans
House: 58 Federalists; 48 Democratic-Republicans
SIXTH CONGRESS (March 4, 1799–March 4, 1801):
Senate: 19 Federalists; 13 Democratic-Republicans
House: 64 Federalists; 42 Democratic-Republicans